Grade 4

Instructional Resources

- Vocabulary Cards
- Activities
- Blackline Masters

Erie, Pennsylvania
BigIdeasLearning.com

Cover Image bgblue/DigitalVision Vectors/Getty Images

Copyright © by Big Ideas Learning, LLC. All rights reserved.

Permission is hereby granted to teachers to reprint or photocopy in classroom quantities only the pages or sheets in this work that carry a Big Ideas Learning copyright notice, provided each copy made shows the copyright notice. These pages are designed to be reproduced by teachers for use in their classes with accompanying Big Ideas Learning material, provided each copy made shows the copyright notice. Such copies may not be sold and further distribution is expressly prohibited. Except as authorized above, prior written permission must be obtained from Big Ideas Learning, LLC to reproduce or transmit this work or portions thereof in any other form or by any other electronic or mechanical means, including but not limited to photocopying and recording, or by any information storage or retrieval system, unless expressly permitted by copyright law. Address inquiries to Permissions, Big Ideas Learning, LLC, 1762 Norcross Road, Erie, PA 16510.

Big Ideas Learning and Big Ideas Math are registered trademarks of Larson Texts, Inc.

Printed in the United States

ISBN 13: 978-1-63736-707-0

23456789–25 24 23 22 21

Contents

Copyright © Big Ideas Learning, LLC.
All rights reserved.

About the Instructional Resources

The Instructional Resources contains a variety of reproducible resources for use throughout the year.

Vocabulary Cards

The Vocabulary Cards in the Student Edition are provided here for quick reference.

Activities

Each chapter activity in the Student Edition is provided here. These games are a fun way for students to practice previously learned skills. Detailed notes about each activity are included at point-of-use in the Teaching Edition.

Blackline Masters

The blackline masters are referenced by name throughout the Student and Teaching Editions. These supports can be reused as needed throughout the year.

Copyright © Big Ideas Learning, LLC.
All rights reserved.

Vocabulary Cards

Copyright © Big Ideas Learning, LLC.
All rights reserved.

Chapter 1 Vocabulary Cards

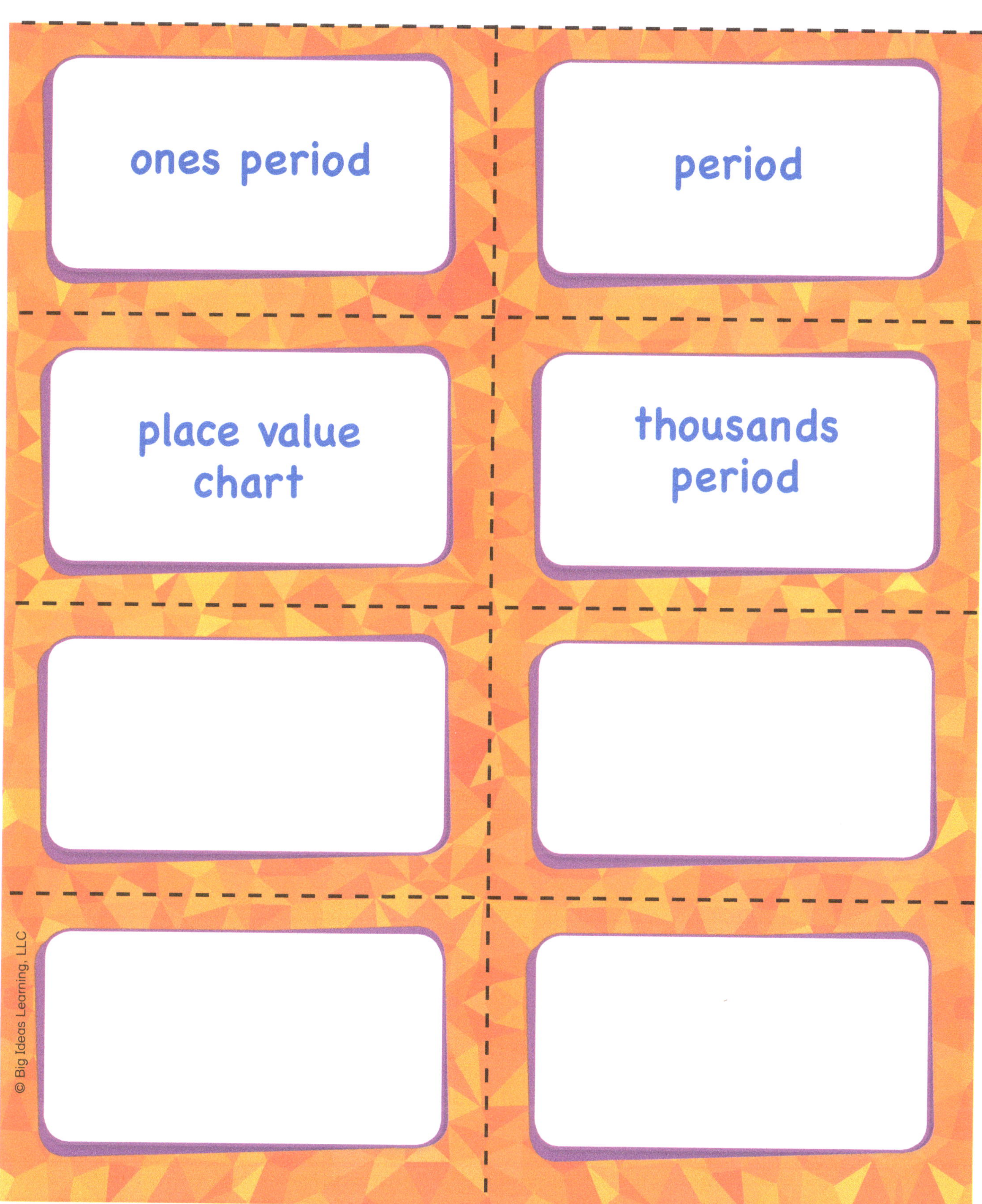

Copyright © Big Ideas Learning, LLC.
All rights reserved.

© Big Ideas Learning, LLC

Each group of three digits separated by commas in a multi-digit number

period period

Thousands Period			Ones Period		
Hundreds	Tens	Ones	Hundreds	Tens	Ones
1	0	0,	0	0	0

© Big Ideas Learning, LLC

The first period in a number

Thousands Period			Ones Period		
Hundreds	Tens	Ones	Hundreds	Tens	Ones
8	1	5,	7	9	6

© Big Ideas Learning, LLC

The period after the ones period in a number

Thousands Period			Ones Period		
Hundreds	Tens	Ones	Hundreds	Tens	Ones
8	1	5,	7	9	6

© Big Ideas Learning, LLC

A chart that shows the value of each digit in a number

Thousands Period			Ones Period		
Hundreds	Tens	Ones	Hundreds	Tens	Ones
2	8	5,	7	4	3

© Big Ideas Learning, LLC

© Big Ideas Learning, LLC

© Big Ideas Learning, LLC

© Big Ideas Learning, LLC

Copyright © Big Ideas Learning, LLC.
All rights reserved.

Chapter 2 Vocabulary Cards

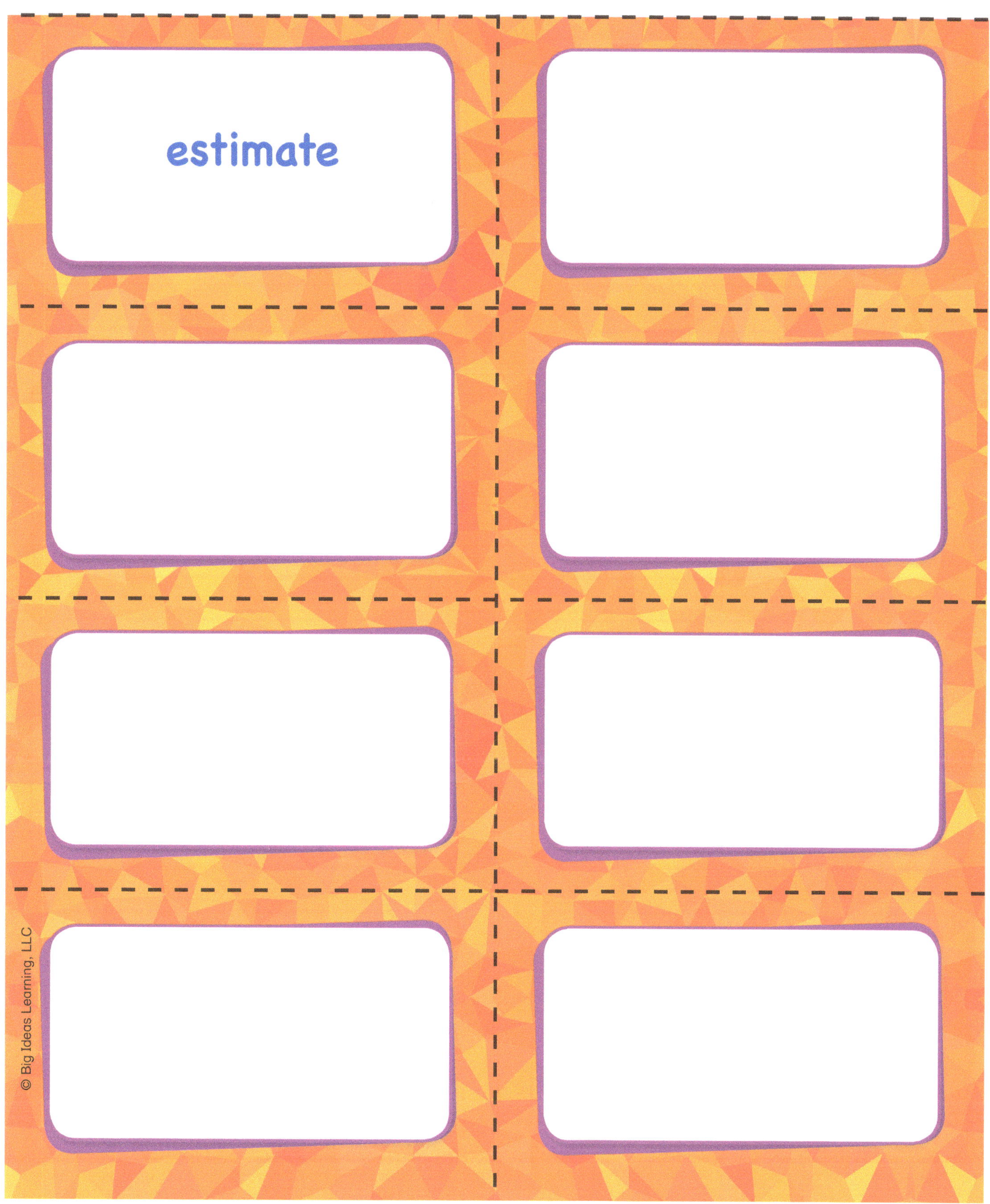

© Big Ideas Learning, LLC

Copyright © Big Ideas Learning, LLC.
All rights reserved.

Copyright © Big Ideas Learning, LLC.
All rights reserved.

Chapter 3 Vocabulary Cards

Copyright © Big Ideas Learning, LLC.
All rights reserved.

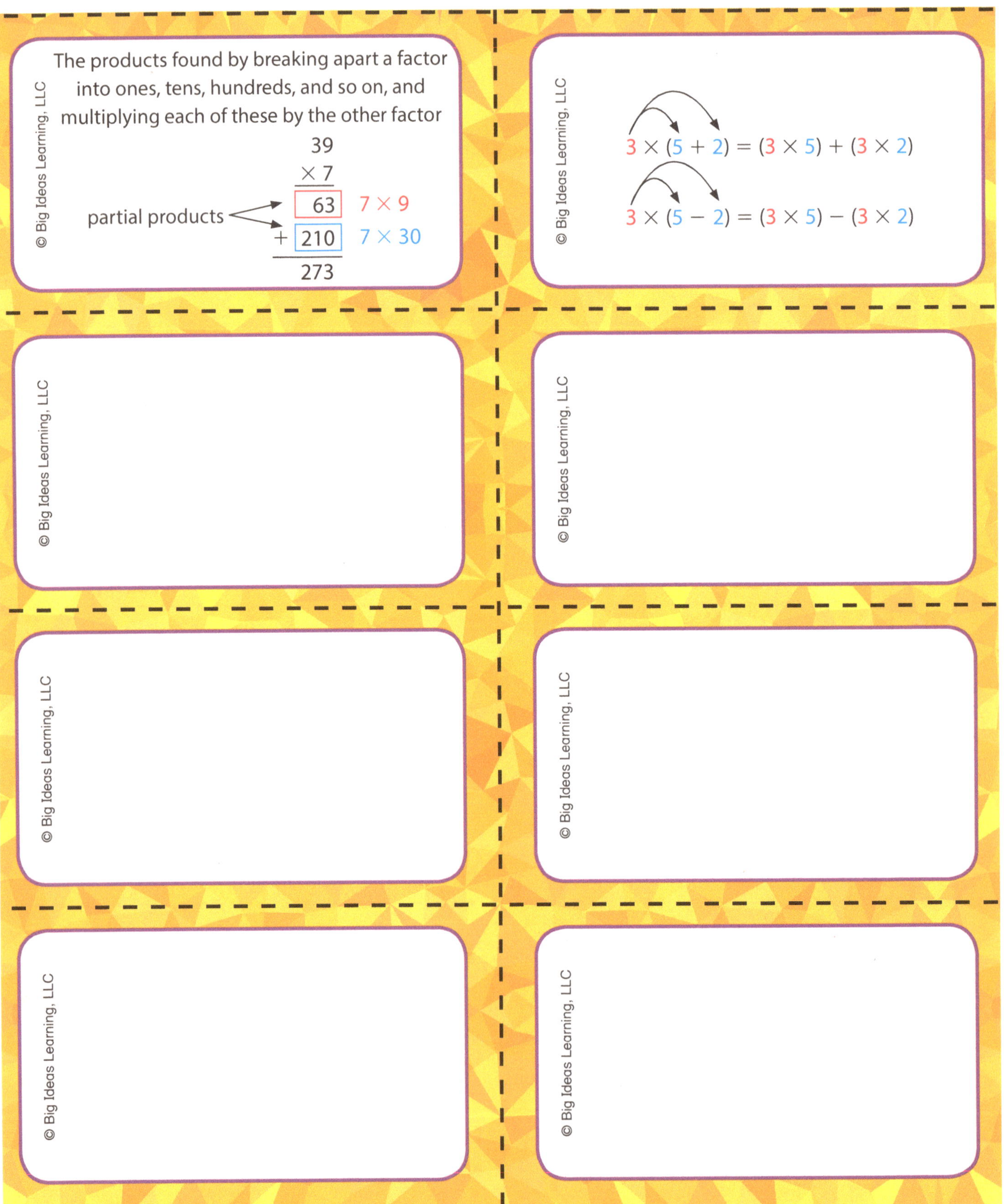

Copyright © Big Ideas Learning, LLC.
All rights reserved.

Chapter 4 Vocabulary Cards

Copyright © Big Ideas Learning, LLC.
All rights reserved.

Copyright © Big Ideas Learning, LLC.
All rights reserved.

Chapter 5 Vocabulary Cards

Copyright © Big Ideas Learning, LLC.
All rights reserved.

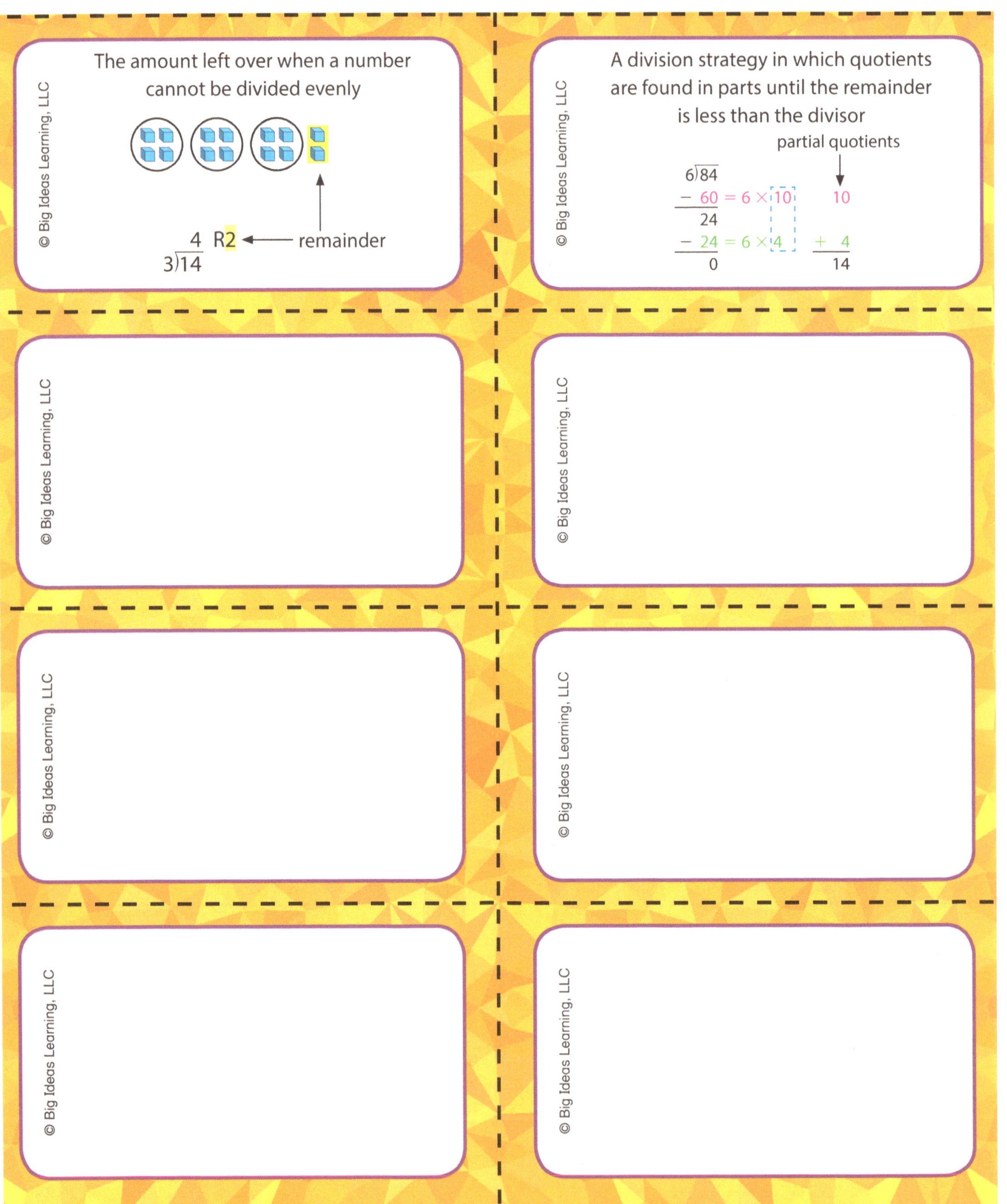

Copyright © Big Ideas Learning, LLC.
All rights reserved.

Chapter 6 Vocabulary Cards

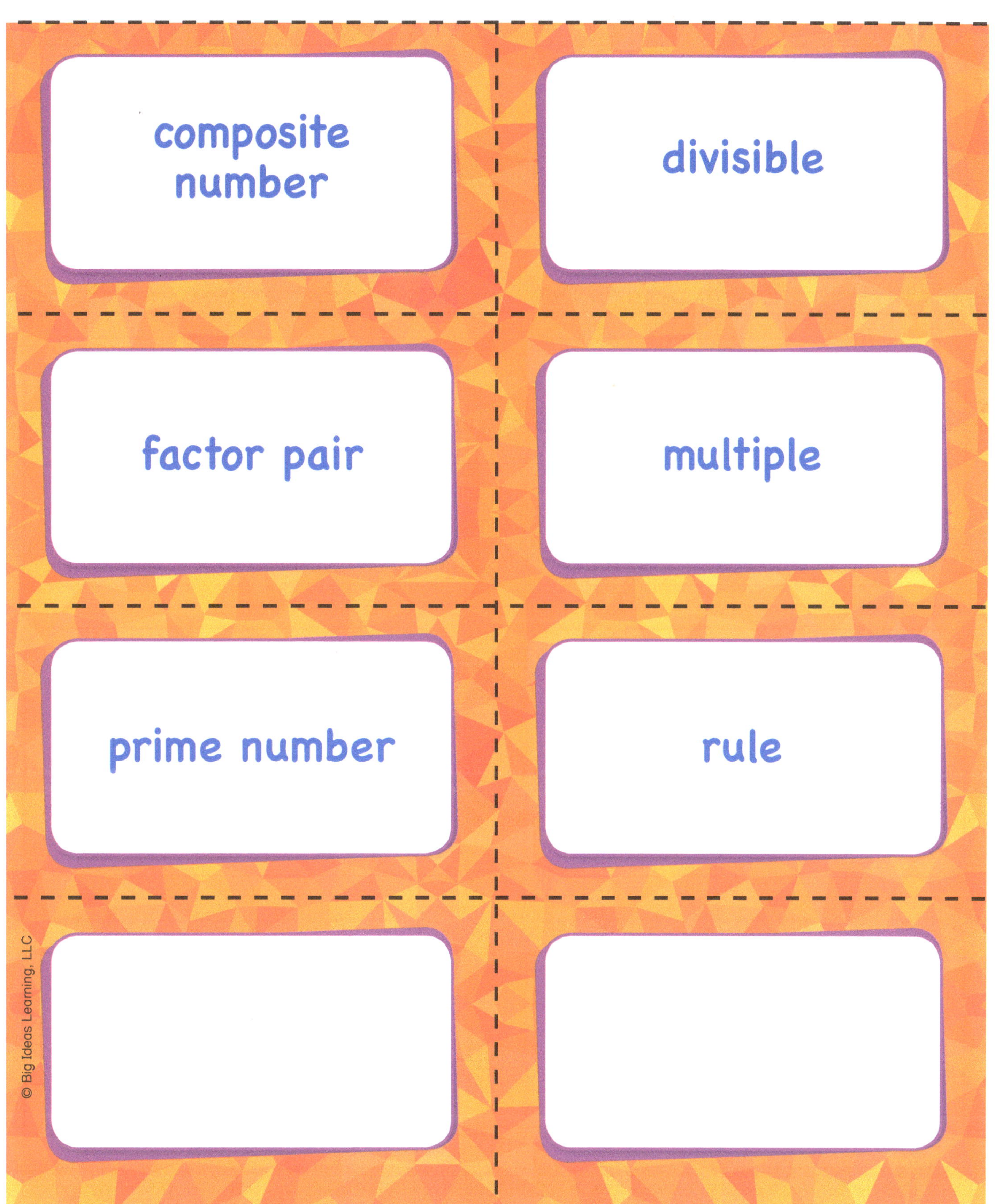

© Big Ideas Learning, LLC

Copyright © Big Ideas Learning, LLC.
All rights reserved.

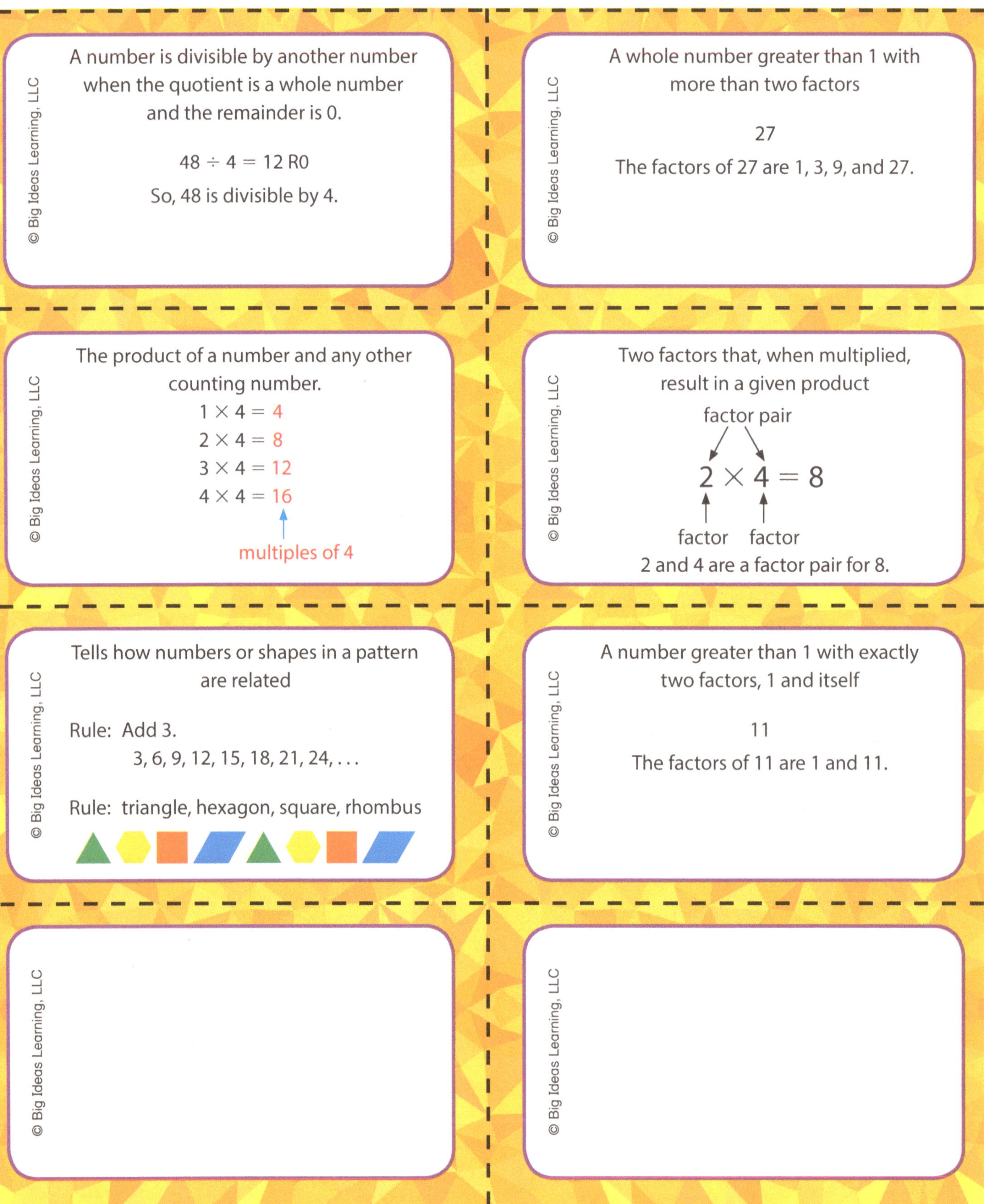

Copyright © Big Ideas Learning, LLC.
All rights reserved.

Chapter 7 Vocabulary Cards

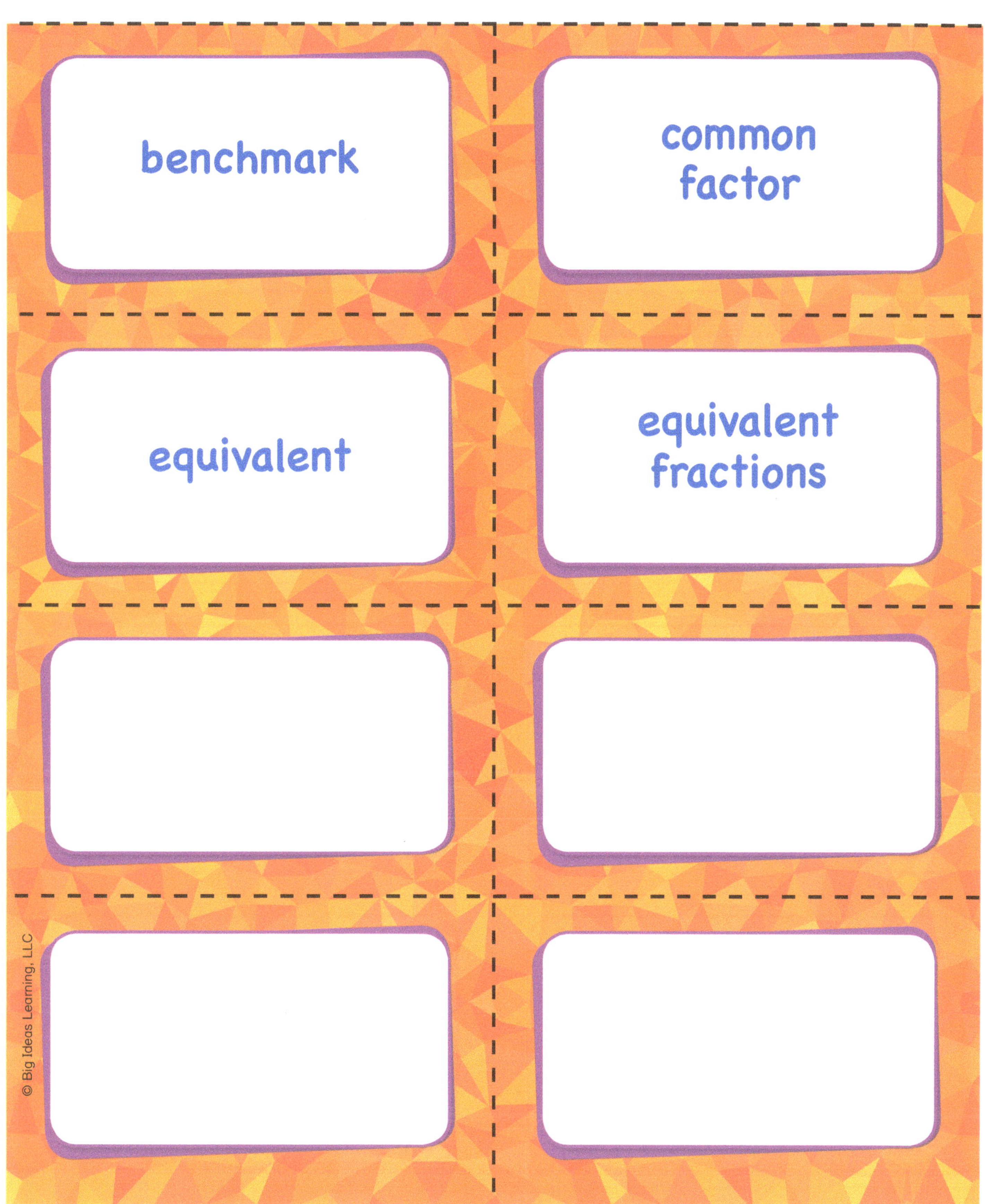

Copyright © Big Ideas Learning, LLC.
All rights reserved.

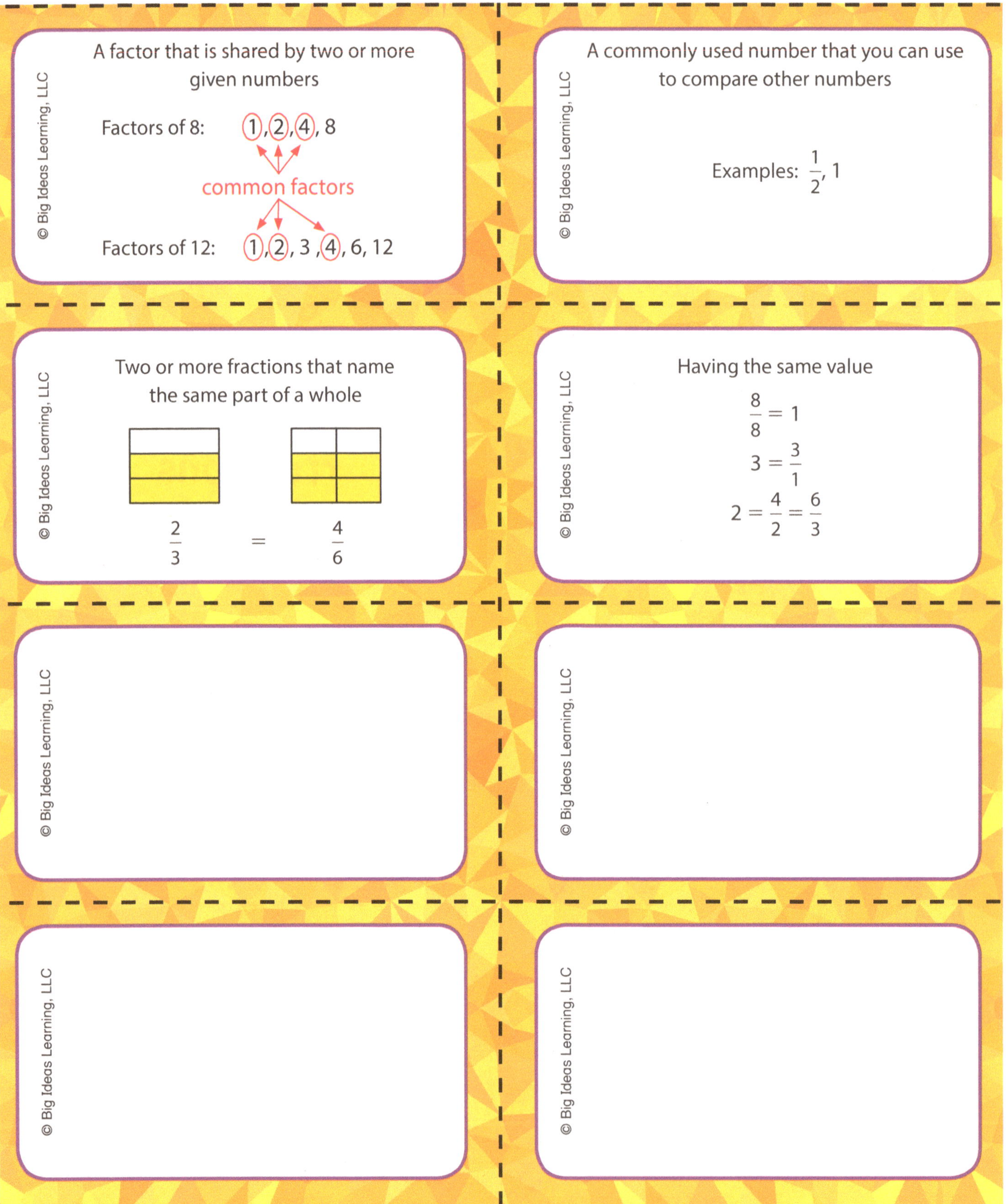

Copyright © Big Ideas Learning, LLC.
All rights reserved.

Chapter 8 Vocabulary Cards

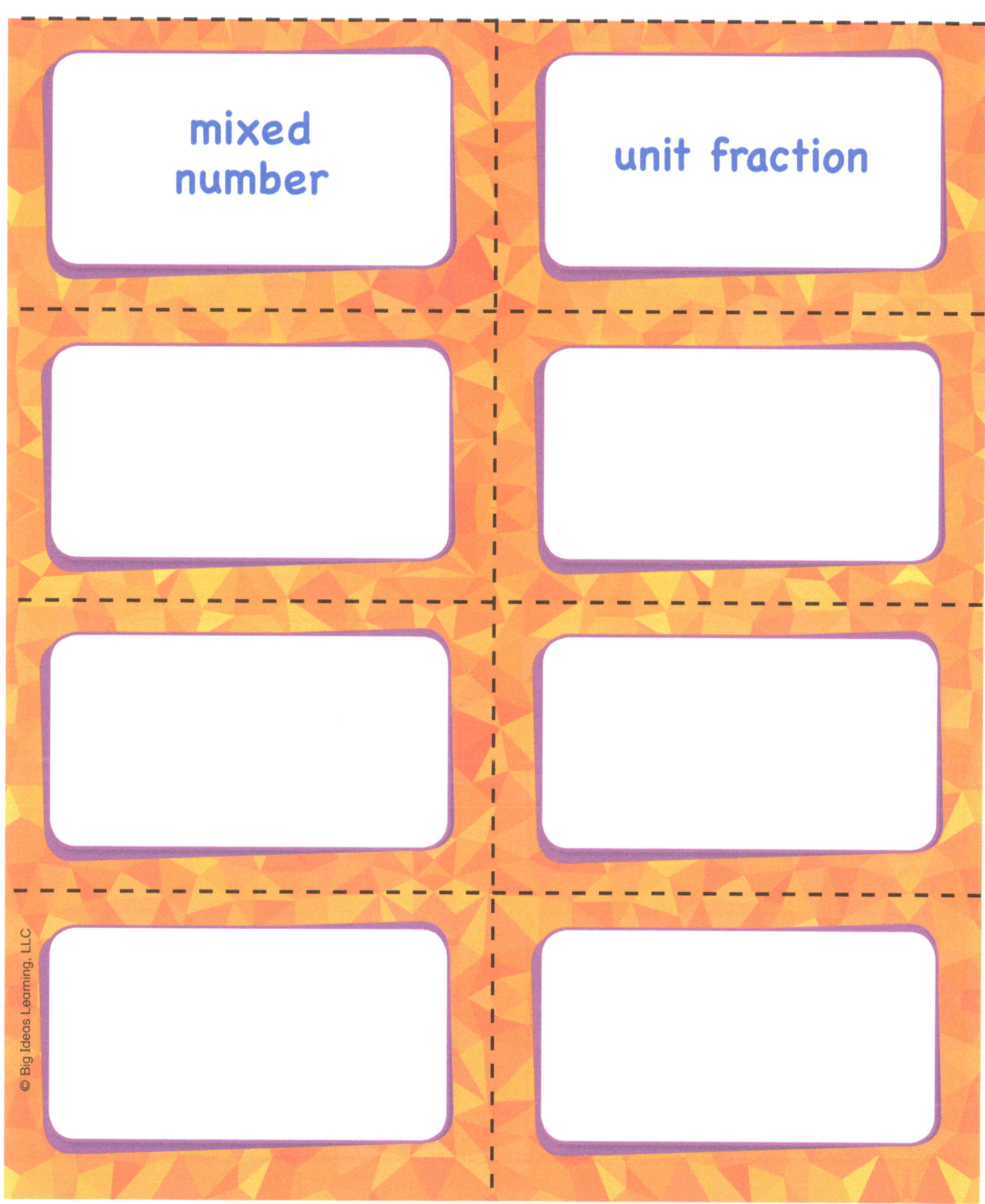

Copyright © Big Ideas Learning, LLC.
All rights reserved.

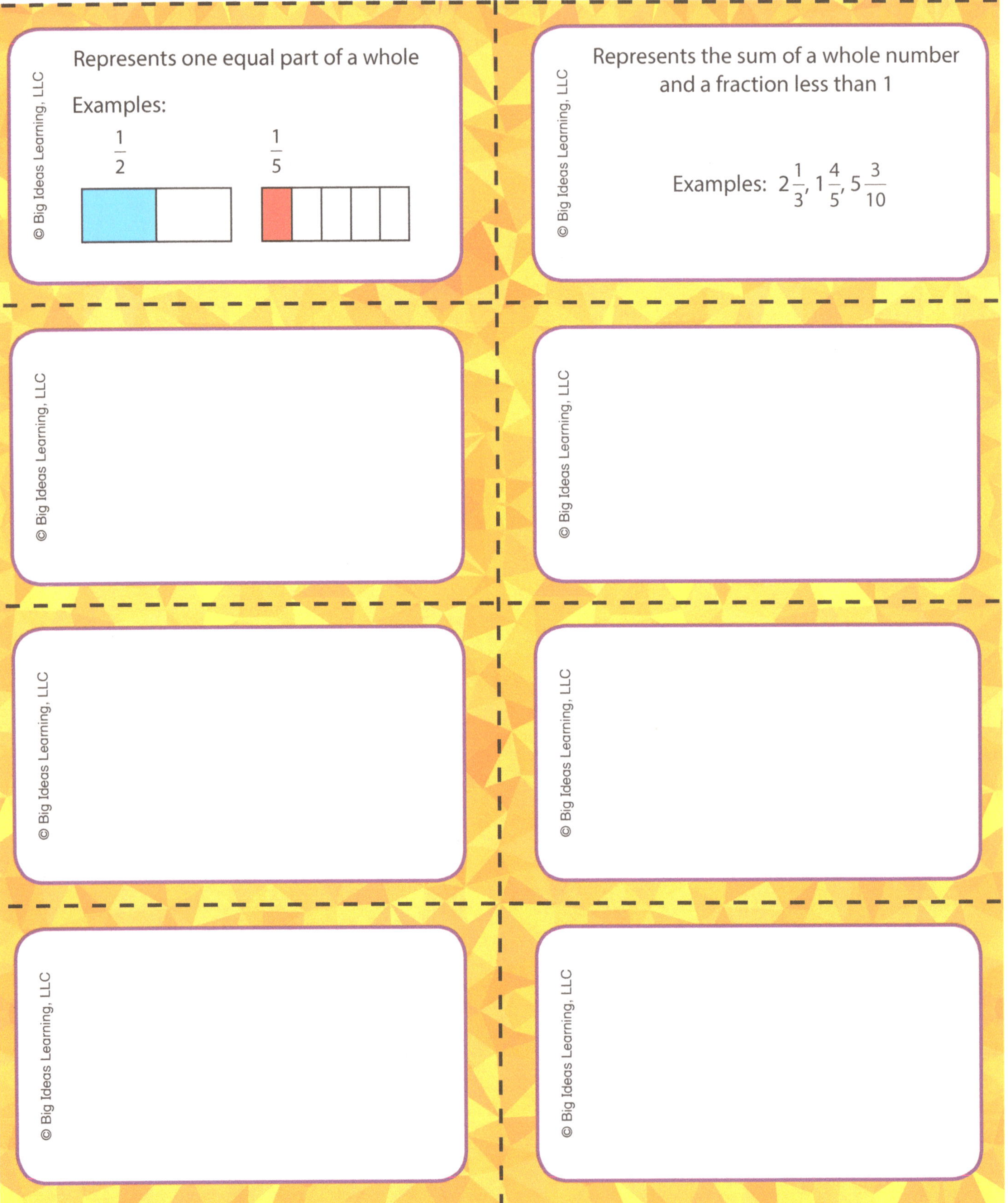

Copyright © Big Ideas Learning, LLC.
All rights reserved.

Chapter 10 Vocabulary Cards

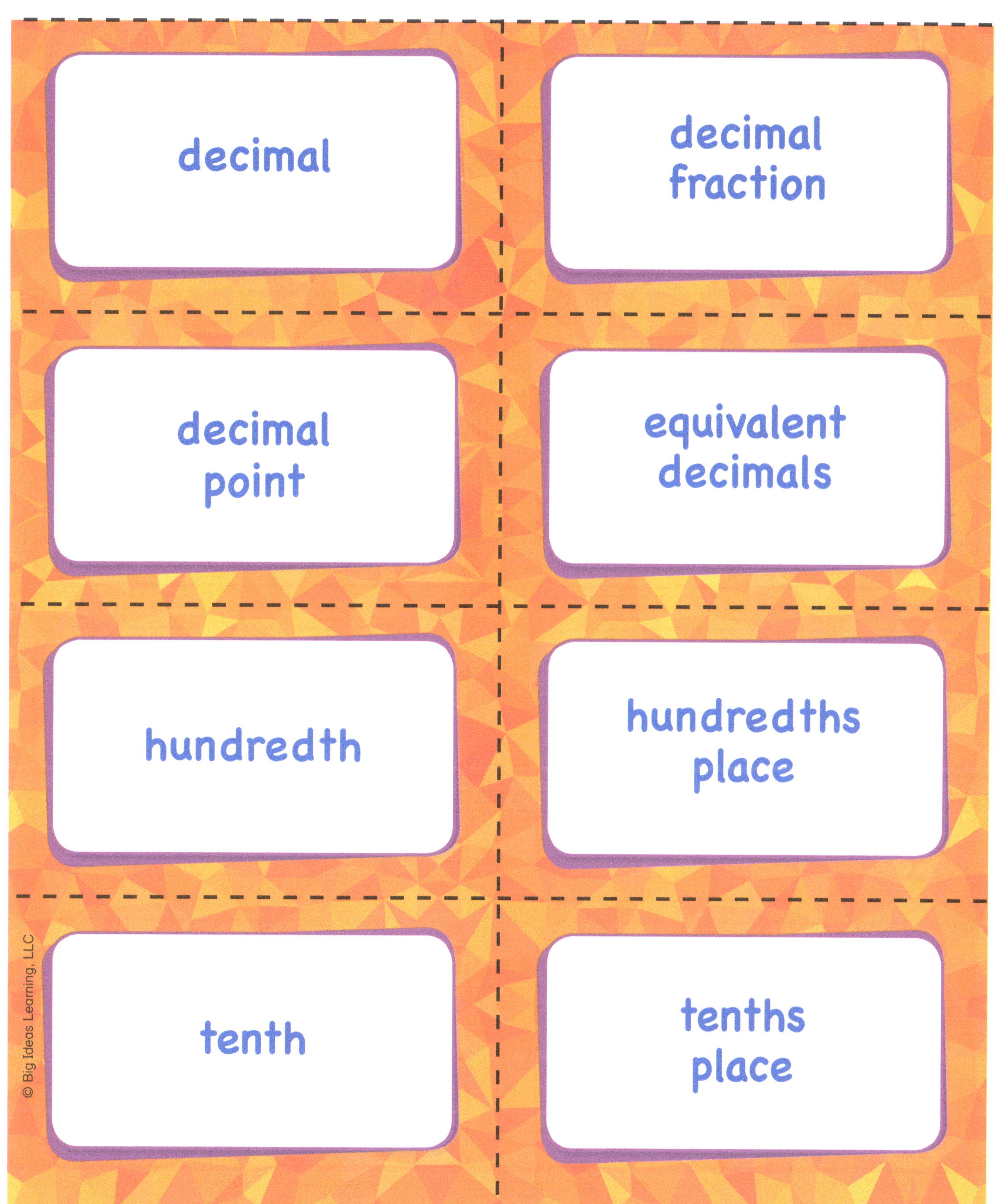

Copyright © Big Ideas Learning, LLC.
All rights reserved.

© Big Ideas Learning, LLC

A fraction with a denominator of 10 or 100

$\frac{26}{100}$

$\frac{9}{10}$

$\frac{60}{100}$

© Big Ideas Learning, LLC

A number with one or more digits to the right of the decimal point

0.3

0.04

0.59

© Big Ideas Learning, LLC

Two or more decimals that have the same value

0.40 = 0.4

© Big Ideas Learning, LLC

A symbol used to separate the ones place and the tenths place in numbers, and to separate the whole dollars and the cents in money

0.1 $5.06

decimal point

© Big Ideas Learning, LLC

The second place to the right of the decimal point

0.01

hundredths place

© Big Ideas Learning, LLC

1 of 100 equal parts of a whole

one hundredth

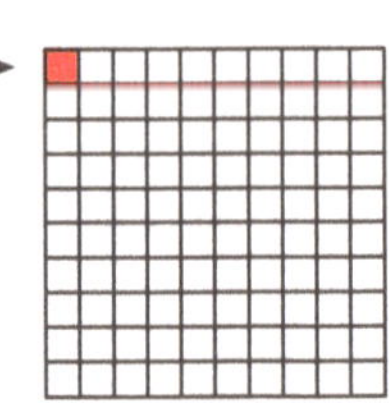

© Big Ideas Learning, LLC

The first place to the right of the decimal point

0.1

tenths place

© Big Ideas Learning, LLC

1 of 10 equal parts of a whole

one tenth

Copyright © Big Ideas Learning, LLC.
All rights reserved.

Chapter 11 Vocabulary Cards

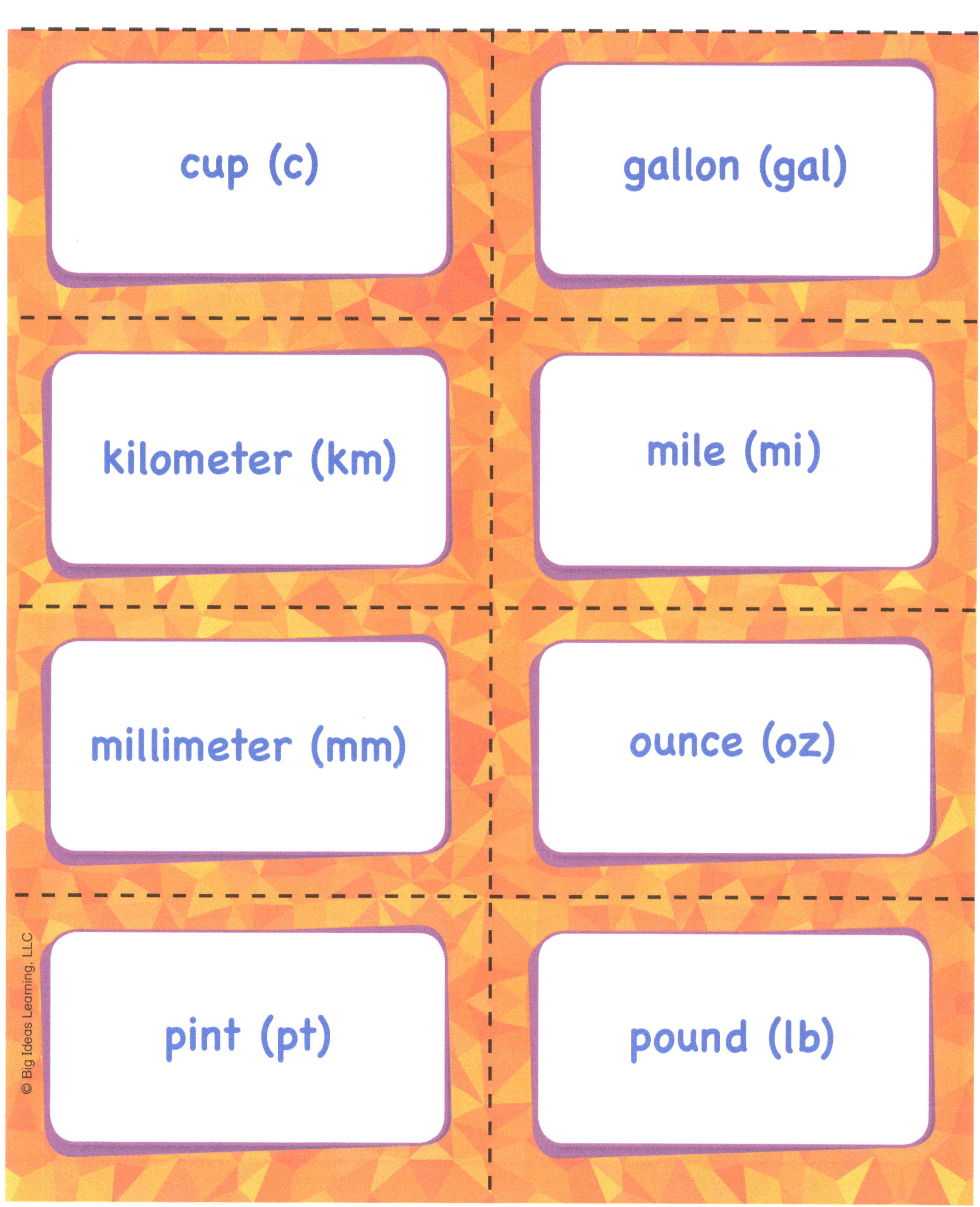

Copyright © Big Ideas Learning, LLC.
All rights reserved.

© Big Ideas Learning, LLC

A customary unit used to measure capacity
There are 4 quarts in 1 gallon.

The capacity of the jug is 1 gallon.

© Big Ideas Learning, LLC

A customary unit used to measure capacity

The capacity of the measuring cup is 1 cup.

© Big Ideas Learning, LLC

A customary unit used to measure length
There are 1,760 yards in 1 mile.

When walking briskly, you can walk 1 mile in about 20 minutes.

© Big Ideas Learning, LLC

A metric unit used to measure length
There are 1,000 meters in 1 kilometer.

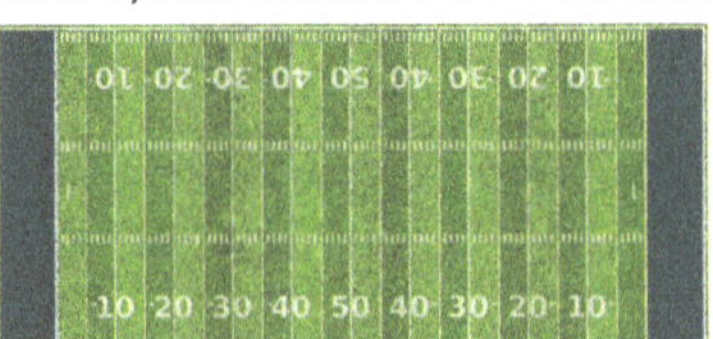

1 kilometer is about the length of 10 football fields including the end zones.

© Big Ideas Learning, LLC

A customary unit used to measure weight

A slice of bread weighs about 1 ounce.

© Big Ideas Learning, LLC

A metric unit used to measure length

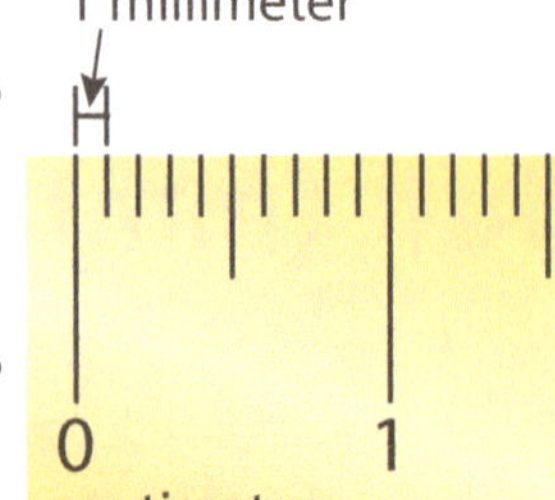

There are 10 millimeters in 1 centimeter.

© Big Ideas Learning, LLC

A customary unit used to measure weight
There are 16 ounces in 1 pound.

A loaf of bread weighs about 1 pound.

© Big Ideas Learning, LLC

A customary unit used to measure capacity
There are 2 cups in 1 pint.

The capacity of the carton is 1 pint.

Copyright © Big Ideas Learning, LLC.
All rights reserved.

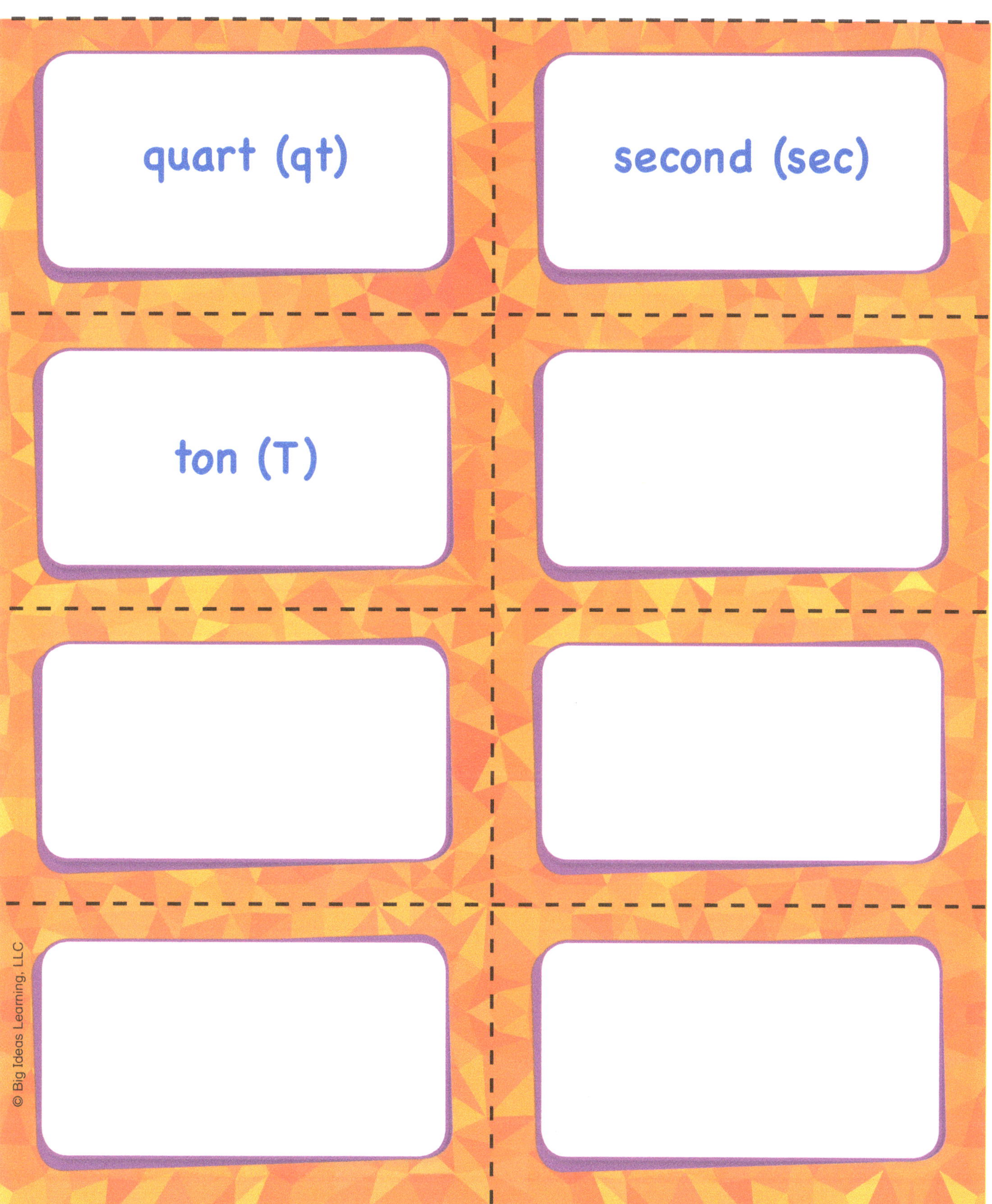

Copyright © Big Ideas Learning, LLC.
All rights reserved.

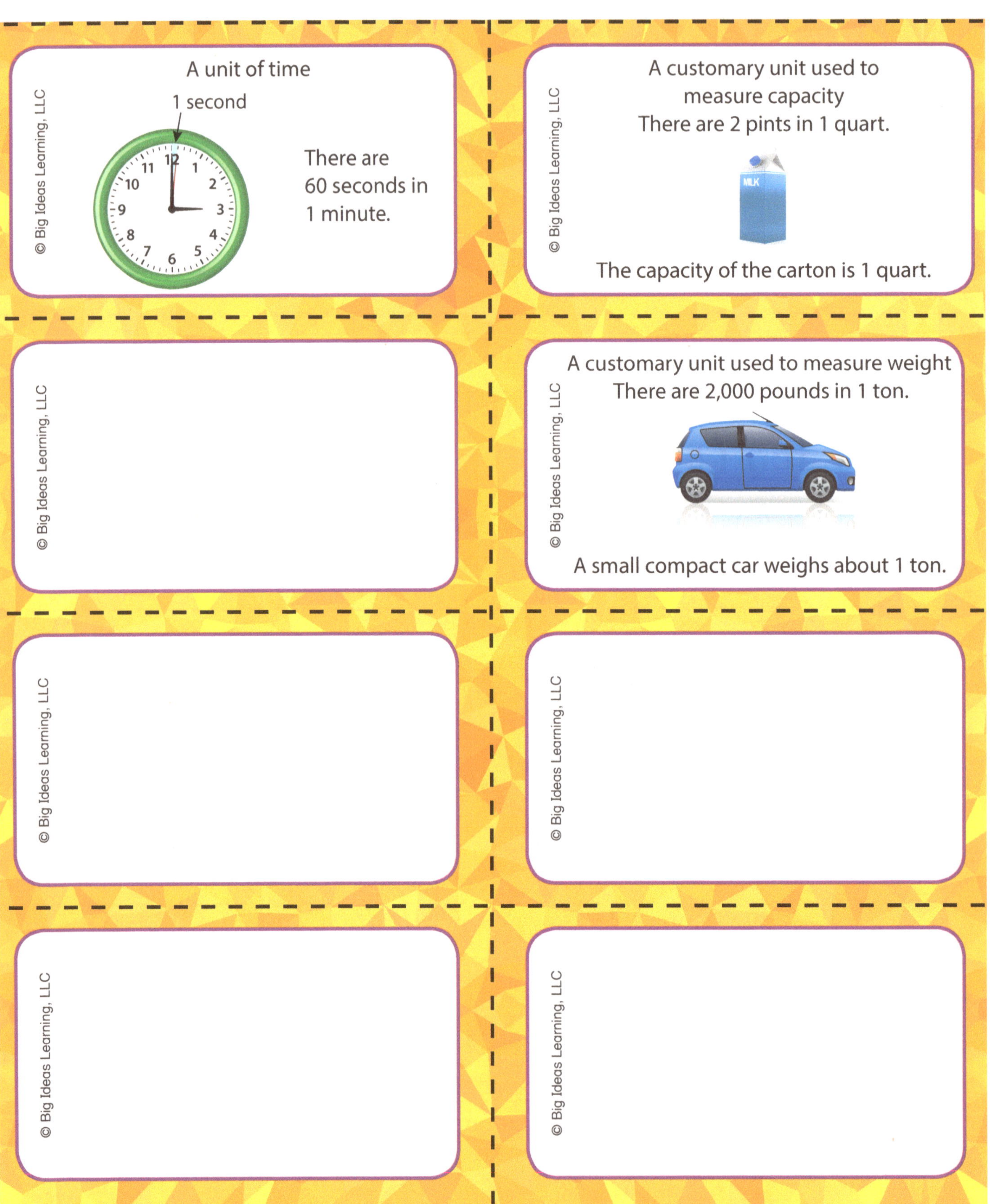

Copyright © Big Ideas Learning, LLC.
All rights reserved.

Chapter 12 Vocabulary Cards

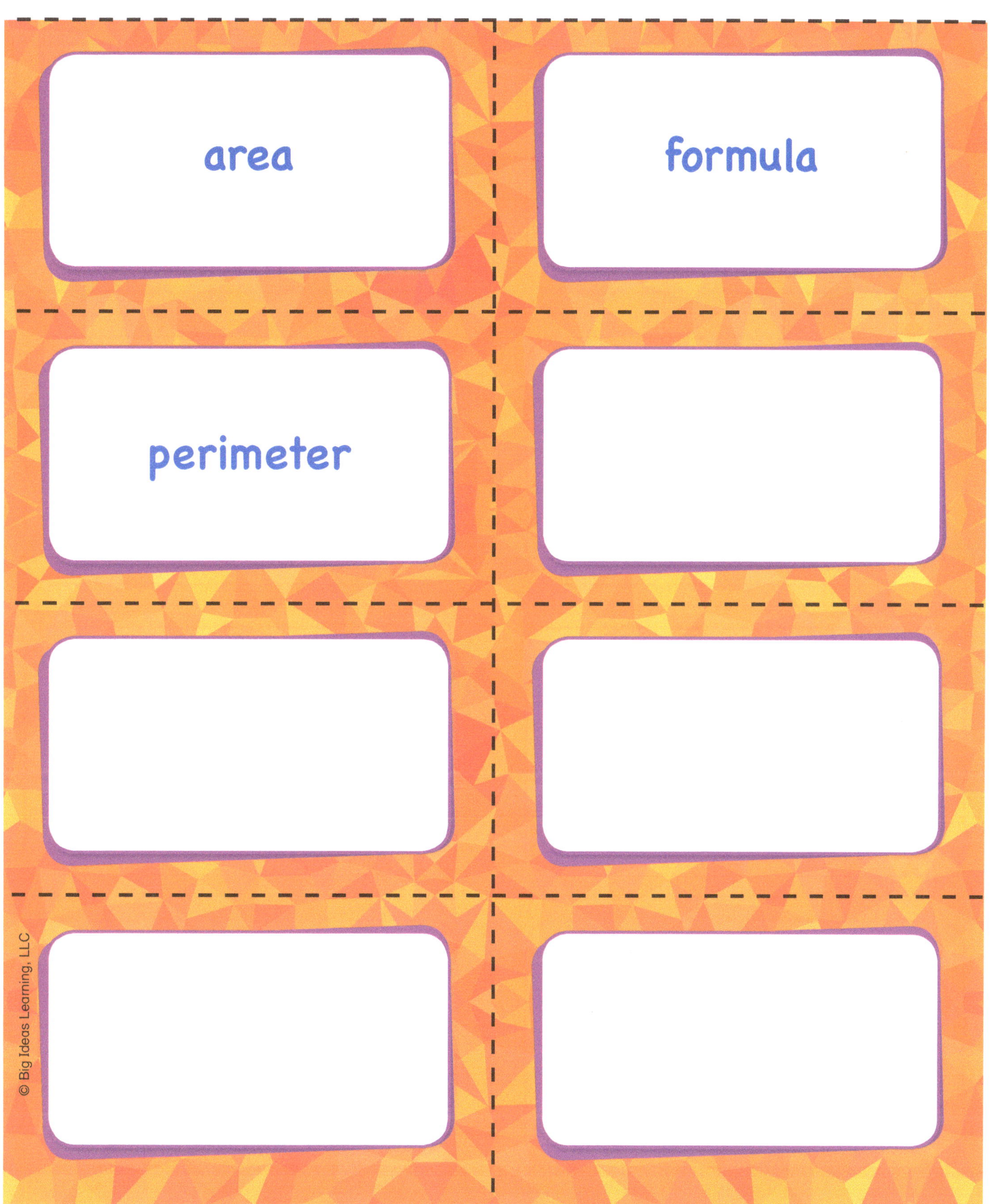

Copyright © Big Ideas Learning, LLC.
All rights reserved.

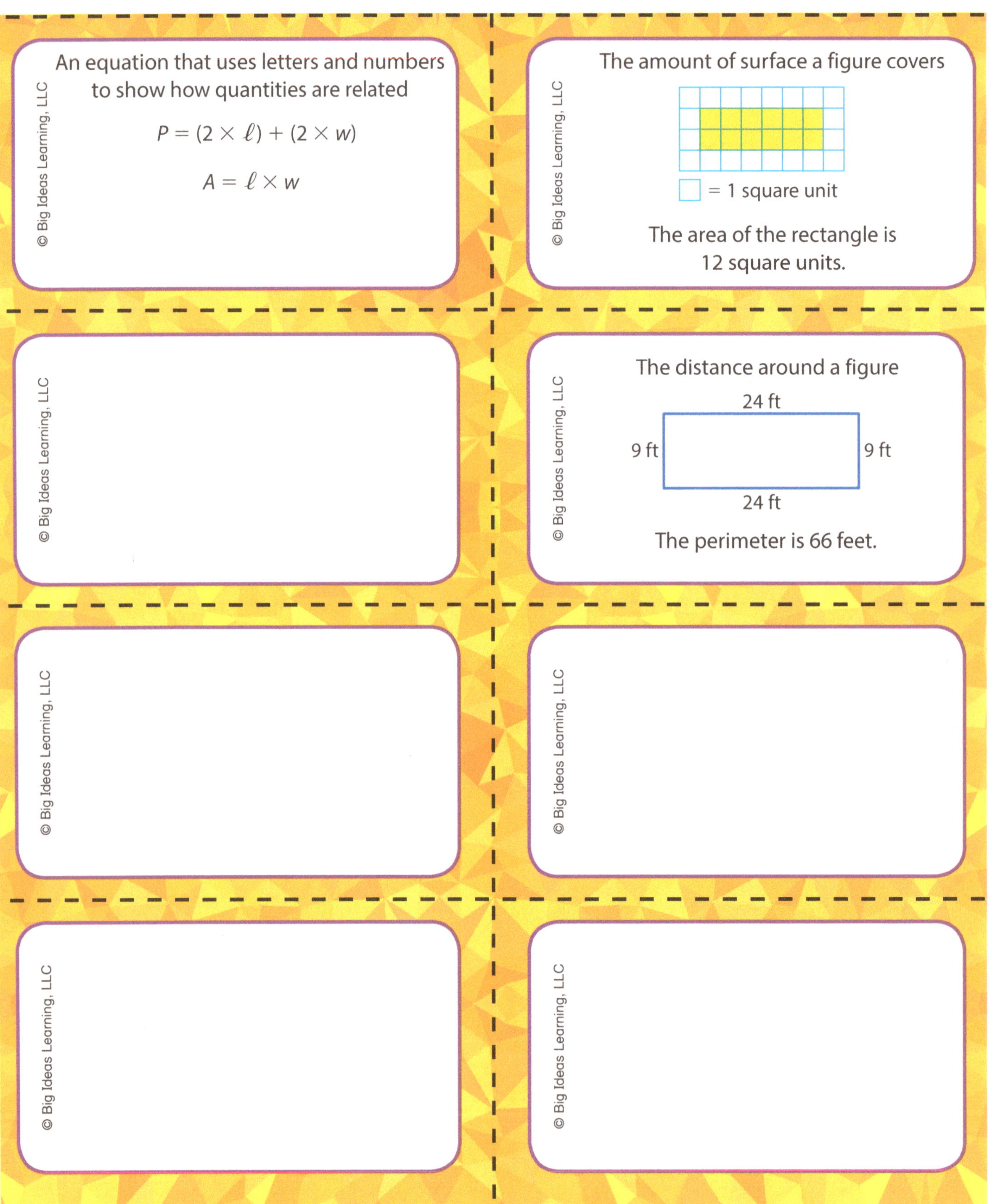

Copyright © Big Ideas Learning, LLC.
All rights reserved.

Chapter 13 Vocabulary Cards

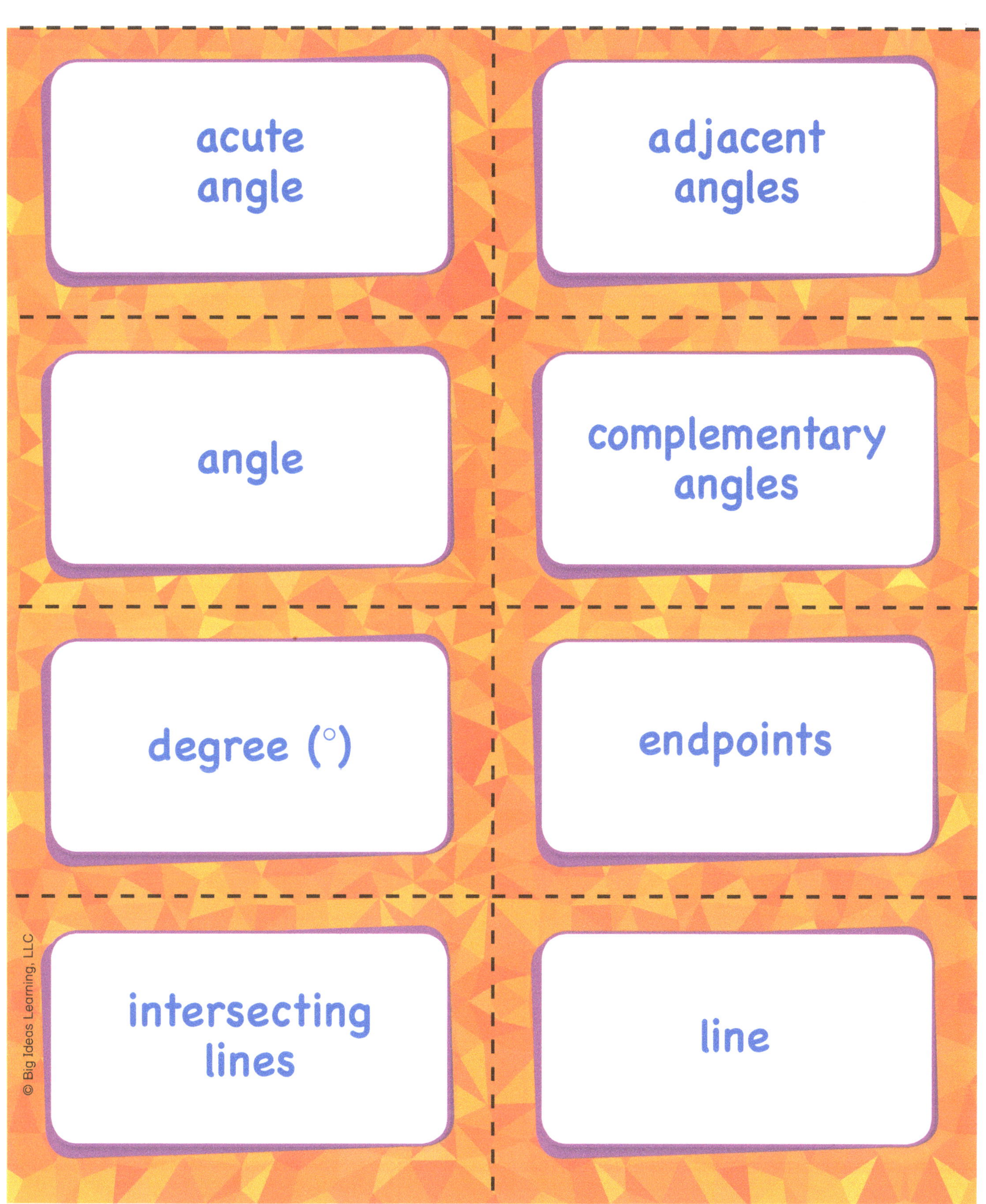

Copyright © Big Ideas Learning, LLC.
All rights reserved.

© Big Ideas Learning, LLC

Two angles that share a common side and a common vertex, but have no other points in common

$\angle ABD$ and $\angle DBC$ are adjacent angles.

© Big Ideas Learning, LLC

An angle that is open less than a right angle

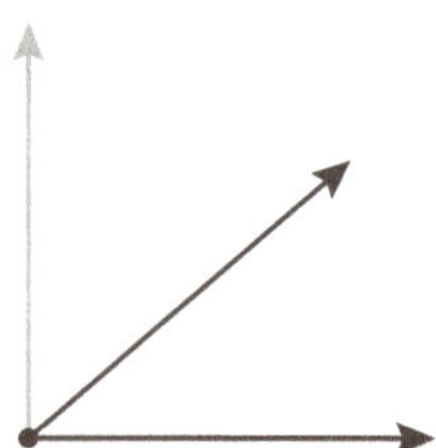

© Big Ideas Learning, LLC

Two angles whose measures have a sum of 90°

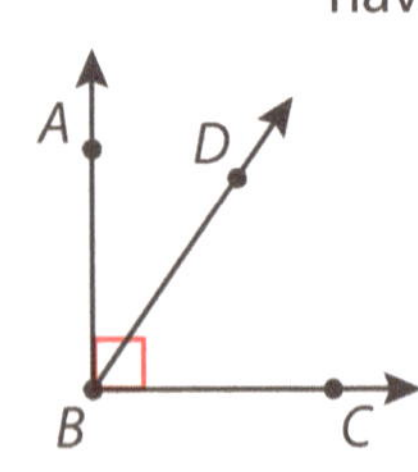

$\angle ABD$ and $\angle DBC$ are complementary angles.

© Big Ideas Learning, LLC

Two rays or line segments that have a common endpoint

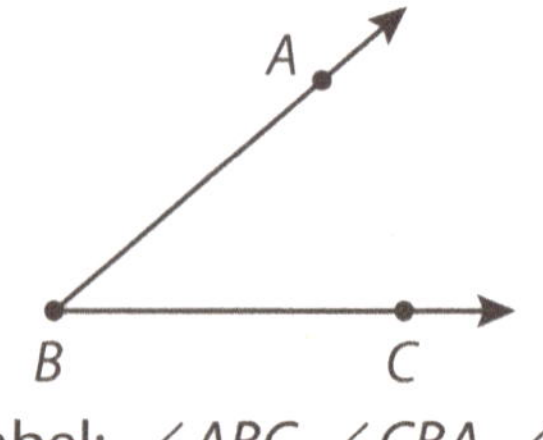

Label: $\angle ABC$, $\angle CBA$, $\angle B$

© Big Ideas Learning, LLC

Points that represent the ends of a line segment or ray

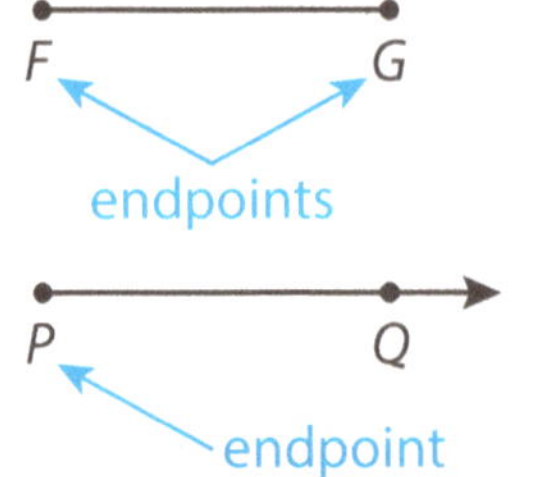

© Big Ideas Learning, LLC

The unit used to measure angles

$1^\circ = \frac{1}{360}$ of a circle

© Big Ideas Learning, LLC

A straight path of points that goes on without end in both directions

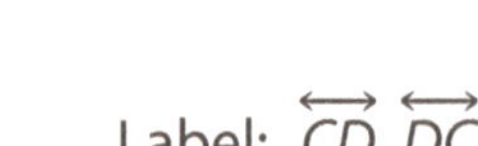

Label: $\overleftrightarrow{CD}$, $\overleftrightarrow{DC}$

© Big Ideas Learning, LLC

Lines that cross at exactly one point

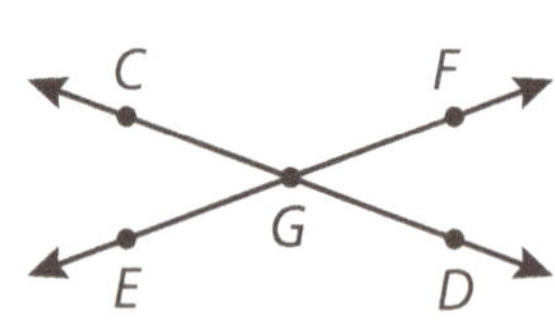

Copyright © Big Ideas Learning, LLC.
All rights reserved.

line segment

obtuse angle

parallel lines

perpendicular lines

point

protractor

ray

right angle

© Big Ideas Learning, LLC

Copyright © Big Ideas Learning, LLC.
All rights reserved.

© Big Ideas Learning, LLC

An angle that is open more than a right angle and less than a straight angle

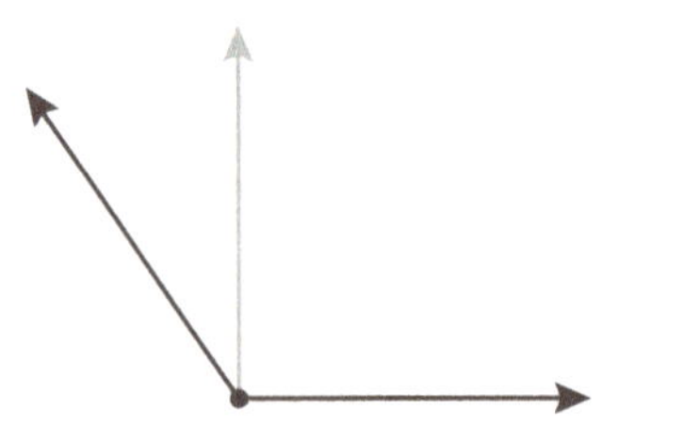

© Big Ideas Learning, LLC

A part of a line that includes two endpoints and all of the points between them

Label: $\overline{FG}, \overline{GF}$

© Big Ideas Learning, LLC

Lines that intersect to form four right angles

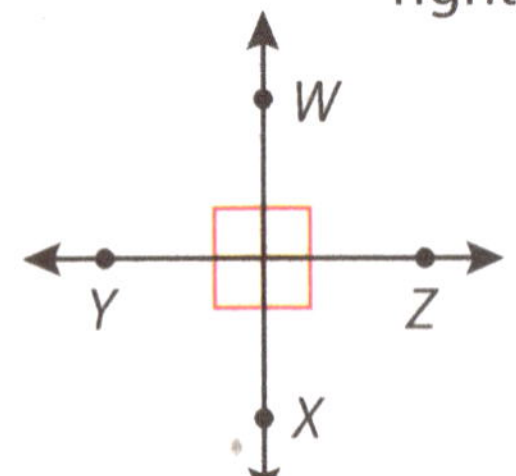

Label: $\overleftrightarrow{WX} \perp \overleftrightarrow{YZ}$

© Big Ideas Learning, LLC

Lines that never intersect

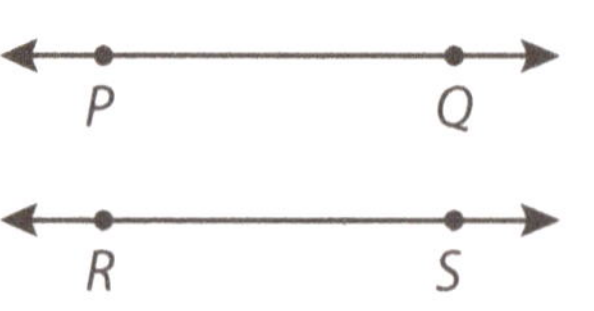

Label: $\overleftrightarrow{PQ} \parallel \overleftrightarrow{RS}$

© Big Ideas Learning, LLC

A tool for measuring and drawing angles

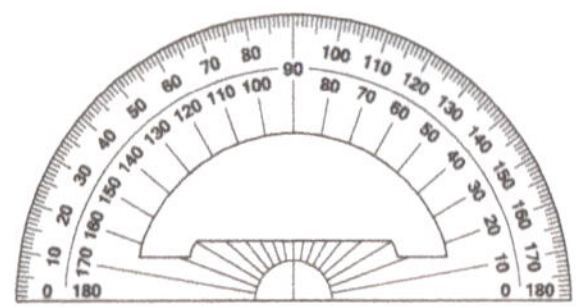

© Big Ideas Learning, LLC

An exact location in space

A

Label: point *A*

© Big Ideas Learning, LLC

An L-shaped angle

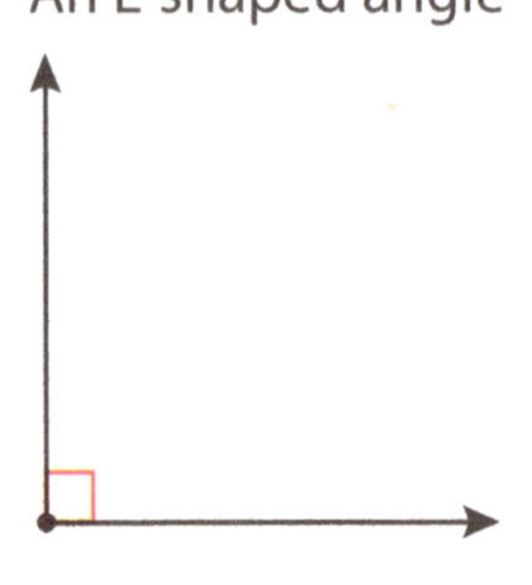

© Big Ideas Learning, LLC

A part of a line that has one endpoint and goes on without end in one direction

Label: $\overrightarrow{PQ}$

Copyright © Big Ideas Learning, LLC.
All rights reserved.

straight angle

supplementary angles

vertex

© Big Ideas Learning, LLC

Copyright © Big Ideas Learning, LLC.
All rights reserved.

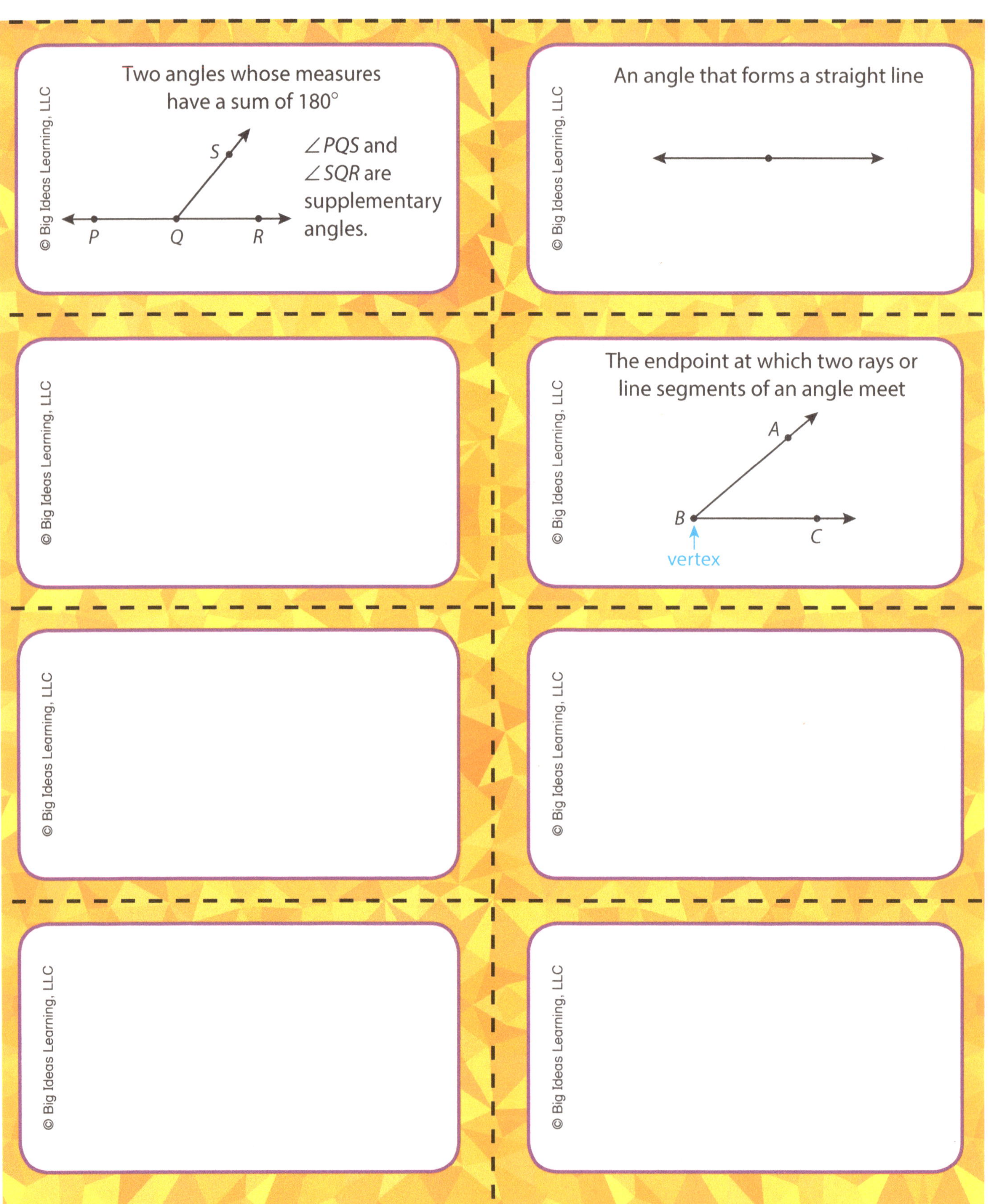

Copyright © Big Ideas Learning, LLC.
All rights reserved.

Chapter 14 Vocabulary Cards

acute triangle

equiangular triangle

equilateral triangle

isosceles triangle

line of symmetry

line symmetry

obtuse triangle

parallelogram

© Big Ideas Learning, LLC

Copyright © Big Ideas Learning, LLC.
All rights reserved.

© Big Ideas Learning, LLC

A triangle that has three angles with the same measure

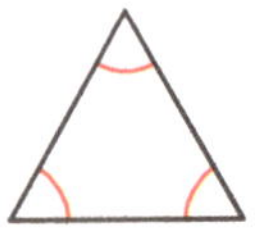

© Big Ideas Learning, LLC

A triangle that has three acute angles

© Big Ideas Learning, LLC

A triangle that has two sides with the same length

© Big Ideas Learning, LLC

A triangle that has three sides with the same length

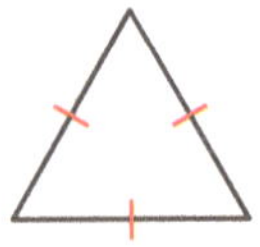

© Big Ideas Learning, LLC

The symmetry that a shape has when it can be folded on a line so that two parts match exactly

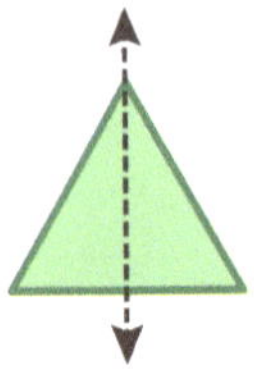

© Big Ideas Learning, LLC

A fold line that divides a shape into two parts that match exactly

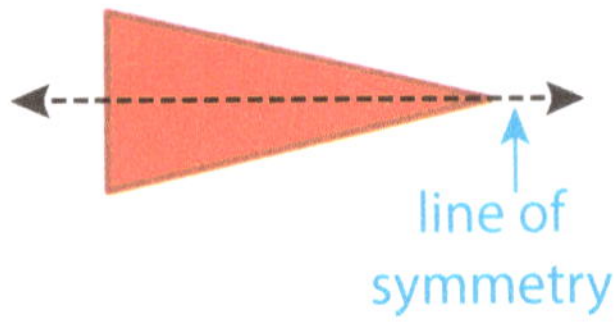

line of symmetry

© Big Ideas Learning, LLC

A quadrilateral that has two pairs of parallel sides

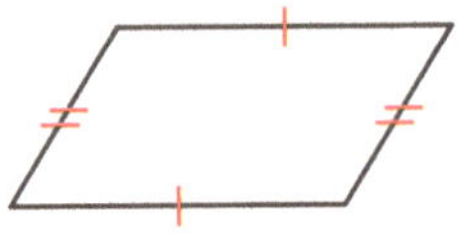

© Big Ideas Learning, LLC

A triangle that has one obtuse angle

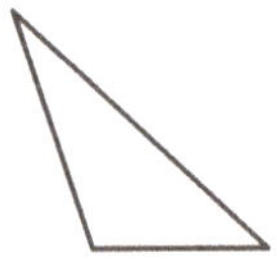

Copyright © Big Ideas Learning, LLC.
All rights reserved.

rectangle

rhombus

right triangle

scalene triangle

square

trapezoid

© Big Ideas Learning, LLC

Copyright © Big Ideas Learning, LLC.
All rights reserved.

© Big Ideas Learning, LLC

A parallelogram that has four sides with the same length

© Big Ideas Learning, LLC

A parallelogram that has four right angles

© Big Ideas Learning, LLC

A triangle that has no sides with the same length

© Big Ideas Learning, LLC

A triangle that has one right angle

© Big Ideas Learning, LLC

A quadrilateral that has exactly one pair of parallel sides

© Big Ideas Learning, LLC

A parallelogram that has four right angles and four sides with the same length

© Big Ideas Learning, LLC

© Big Ideas Learning, LLC

Copyright © Big Ideas Learning, LLC.
All rights reserved.

Activities

Copyright © Big Ideas Learning, LLC.
All rights reserved.

Place Value Plug In

Directions:

1. Players take turns.
2. On your turn, roll six dice. Arrange the dice into a six-digit number that matches one of the descriptions.
3. Write your number on the lines.
4. The first player to complete all of the numbers wins!

A number with...	Number
6 in the tens place 2 in the ten thousands place	___ ___ ___ , ___ ___ ___
4 in the ones place 5 in the thousands place	___ ___ ___ , ___ ___ ___
3 in the tens place 1 in the hundreds place	___ ___ ___ , ___ ___ ___
5 in the ones place 2 in the hundred thousands place	___ ___ ___ , ___ ___ ___
4 in the thousands place 6 in the ten thousands place	___ ___ ___ , ___ ___ ___
three of the same digit	___ ___ ___ , ___ ___ ___
digits in the hundred thousands place and ones place have a sum of 8	___ ___ ___ , ___ ___ ___
digits in the hundreds place and ten thousands place have a sum of 7	___ ___ ___ , ___ ___ ___
FREEBIE! Use any number!	___ ___ ___ , ___ ___ ___

Copyright © Big Ideas Learning, LLC.
All rights reserved.

Race to the Moon

Directions:

1. Players take turns.
2. On your turn, flip a Race for the Moon Card and find the sum or difference.
3. Move your piece to the next number on the board that is highlighted in your answer.

Copyright © Big Ideas Learning, LLC.
All rights reserved.

Multiplication Quest

Directions:

1. Players take turns rolling a die. Players solve problems on their boards to race the knights to their castles.
2. On your turn, solve the next multiplication problem in the row of your roll.
3. The first player to get a knight to a castle wins!

Roll				
1	7×8	32×3	629×4	$5{,}107 \times 6$
2	3×9	56×4	248×1	$3{,}816 \times 8$
3	5×2	81×5	921×9	$7{,}249 \times 7$
4	4×6	90×9	455×8	$9{,}683 \times 2$
5	8×1	12×7	806×3	$4{,}749 \times 5$
6	6×7	79×2	573×6	$8{,}106 \times 4$

Copyright © Big Ideas Learning, LLC.
All rights reserved.

Multiplication Boss

Directions:

1. Each player flips 4 Number Cards and uses them in any order to create a multiplication problem with two-digit factors.
2. Each player finds the product of the two factors.
3. Players compare products. The player with the greater product takes all 8 cards.
4. If the products are equal, each player flips 4 more cards and plays again. The player with the greater product takes all 16 cards.
5. The player with the most cards at the end of the round wins!

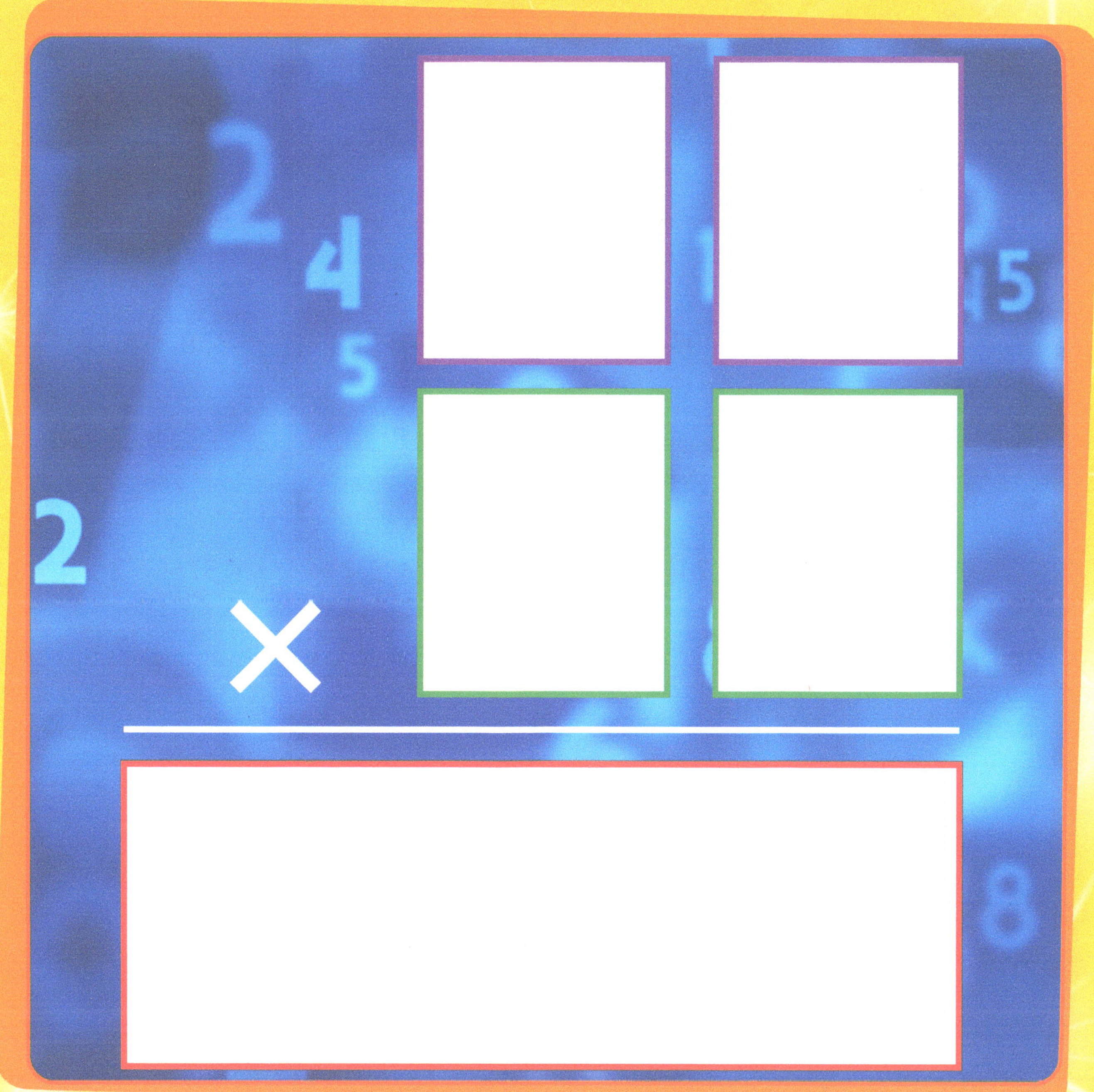

Copyright © Big Ideas Learning, LLC.
All rights reserved.

Division Dots

Directions:

1. Players take turns connecting two dots, each using a different color.
2. On your turn, connect two dots, vertically or horizontally. If you close a square around a division problem, find and write the quotient and the remainder. If you do not close a square, your turn is over.
3. Continue playing until all division problems are solved.
4. The player with the most completed squares wins!

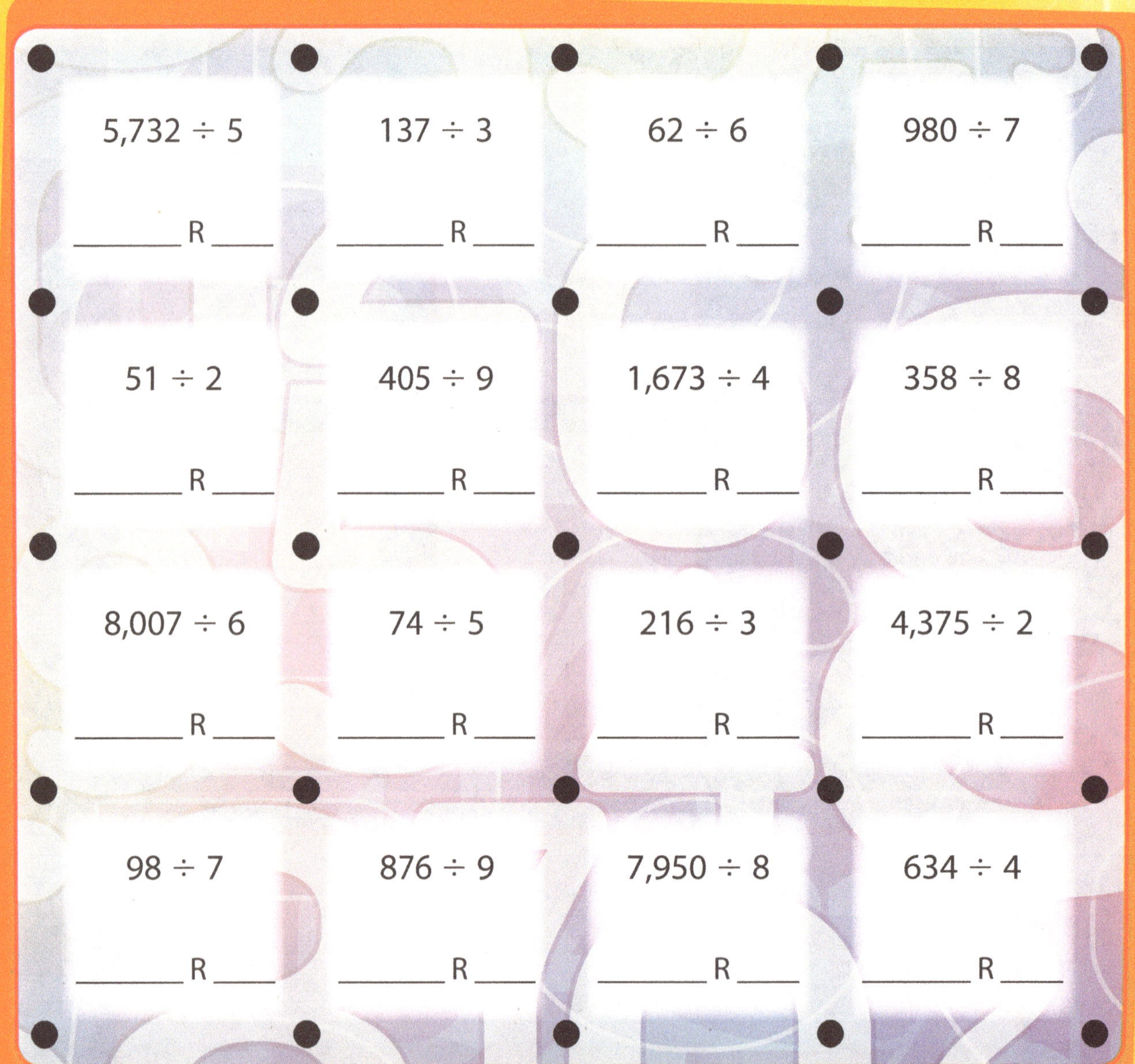

$5{,}732 \div 5$ _____ R ____	$137 \div 3$ _____ R ____	$62 \div 6$ _____ R ____	$980 \div 7$ _____ R ____
$51 \div 2$ _____ R ____	$405 \div 9$ _____ R ____	$1{,}673 \div 4$ _____ R ____	$358 \div 8$ _____ R ____
$8{,}007 \div 6$ _____ R ____	$74 \div 5$ _____ R ____	$216 \div 3$ _____ R ____	$4{,}375 \div 2$ _____ R ____
$98 \div 7$ _____ R ____	$876 \div 9$ _____ R ____	$7{,}950 \div 8$ _____ R ____	$634 \div 4$ _____ R ____

Copyright © Big Ideas Learning, LLC.
All rights reserved.

Multiple Lineup

Directions:

1. Players take turns rolling a die.
2. On your turn, place a counter on a multiple of the number of your roll. If there is not a multiple of the number of your roll, you lose your turn.
3. The first player to create a line of 5 in a row, horizontally, vertically, or diagonally, wins!

30	18	9	16	36
15	4	10	44	17
25	42	7	80	21
6	75	22	45	56
11	27	12	95	24

Copyright © Big Ideas Learning, LLC.
All rights reserved.

Fraction Boss

Directions:

1. Divide the Fraction Boss Cards equally between both players.
2. Each player flips a Fraction Boss Card.
3. Players compare their fractions. The player with the greater fraction takes both cards.
4. If the fractions are equal, each player flips another card. Players compare their fractions. The player with the greater fraction takes all four cards.
5. The player with the most cards at the end of the round wins!

Player A	Player B

Copyright © Big Ideas Learning, LLC.
All rights reserved.

Three In a Row: Fraction Add or Subtract

Directions:

1. Players take turns.
2. On your turn, spin both spinners. Choose whether to add or subtract.
3. Add or subtract the mixed number and fraction. Cover the sum or difference.
4. If the sum or difference is already covered, you lose your turn.
5. The first player to get three in a row wins!

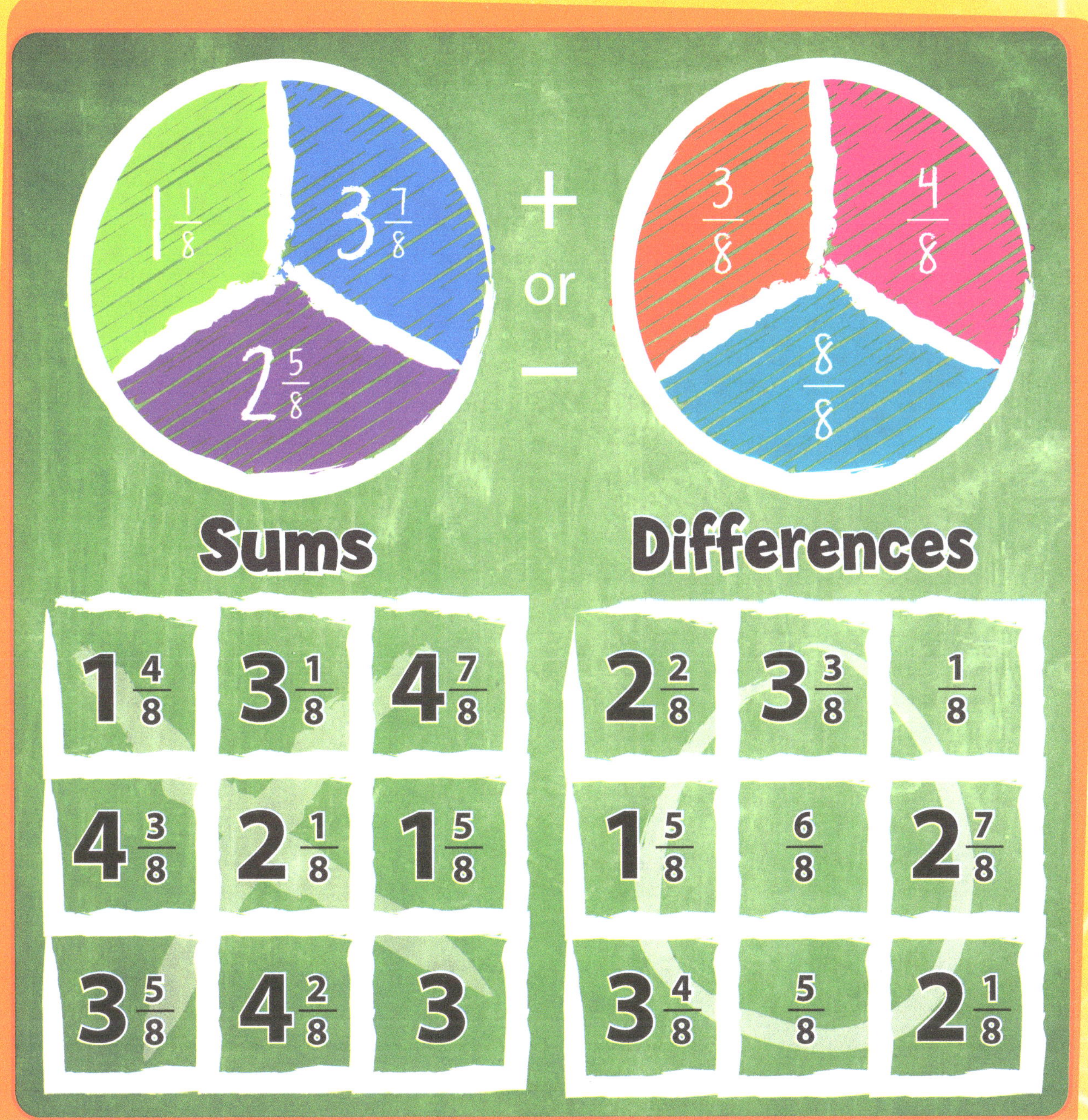

Copyright © Big Ideas Learning, LLC.
All rights reserved.

Three In a Row: Fraction Multiplication

Directions:

1. Players take turns.
2. On your turn, spin both spinners.
3. Multiply the whole number and the fraction or mixed number. Cover the product.
4. If the product is already covered, you lose your turn.
5. The first player to get three in a row wins!

Copyright © Big Ideas Learning, LLC.
All rights reserved.

Decimal Boss

Directions:

1. Divide the Decimal Boss Cards equally between both players.
2. Each player flips a Decimal Boss Card.
3. Players compare their numbers. The player with the greater number takes both cards.
4. The player with the most cards at the end of the round wins!

Player A	Player B

Copyright © Big Ideas Learning, LLC.
All rights reserved.

Conversion Flip and Find

Directions:

1. Choose which conversion cards you will play with.
2. Place the cards face down on the board.
3. Players take turns flipping two cards.
4. If your two cards show equivalent measures, keep the cards.
   If your cards show different measures, flip the cards back over.
5. The player with the most matches wins!

Copyright © Big Ideas Learning, LLC.
All rights reserved.

Area Roll and Conquer

Directions:

1. Players take turns rolling two dice.
2. On your turn, create a rectangle with the numbers on the dice as the length and width. Your rectangle cannot cover another rectangle.
3. Shade the rectangle in your color. Record the multiplication equation for the rectangle.
4. If you cannot create a rectangle on the board, then you lose your turn. Play 10 rounds, if possible.
5. The player with the greatest area covered wins!

Example:

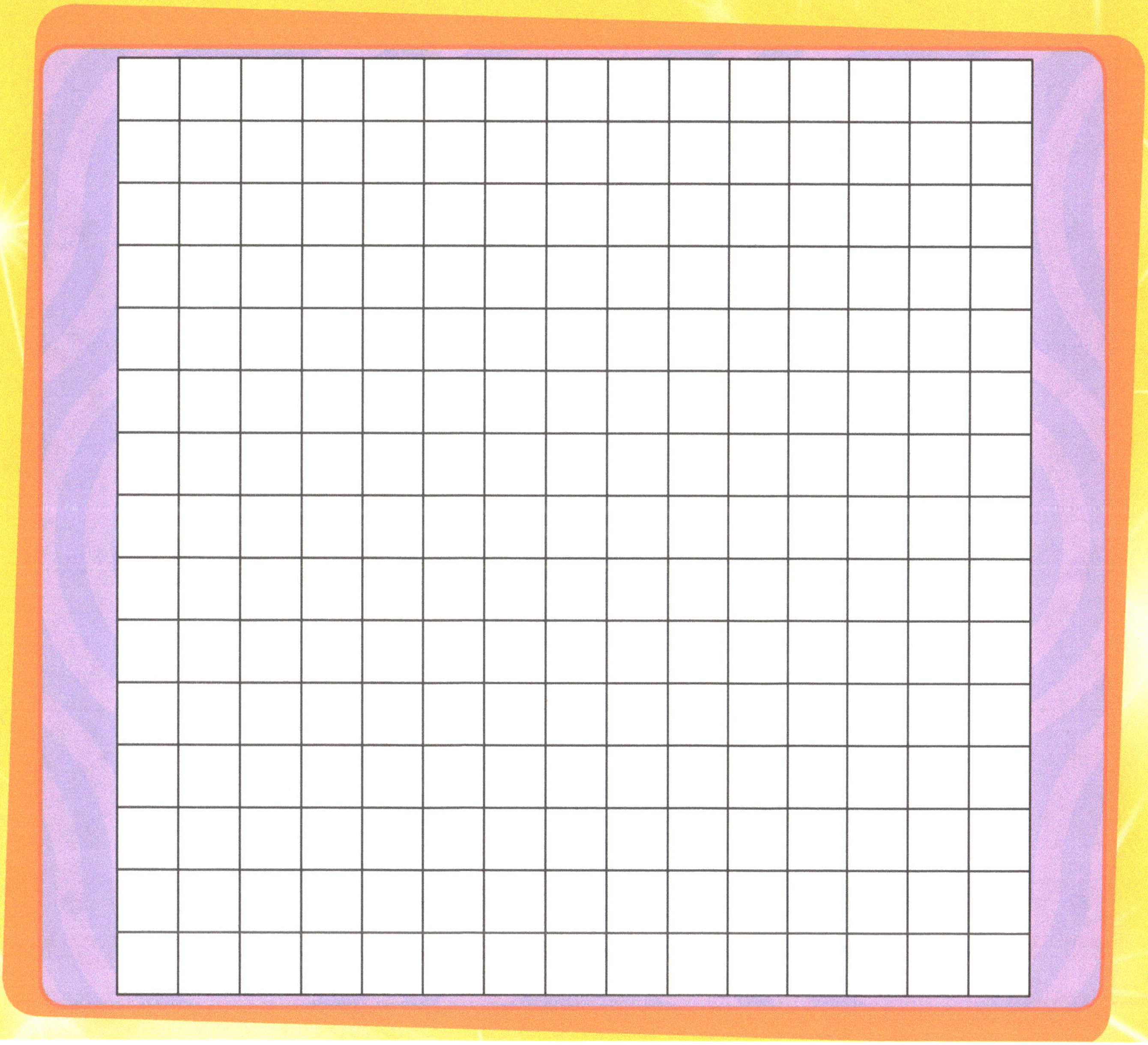

Copyright © Big Ideas Learning, LLC.
All rights reserved.

Geometry Dots

Directions:

1. Players take turns connecting two dots, each using a different color.
2. On your turn, connect two dots, vertically or horizontally. If you close a square around an angle, find the measure of the angle inside the square. If you do not close a square, your turn is over.
3. Continue playing until you find all of the angle measures.
4. The player that finds the most angle measures wins!

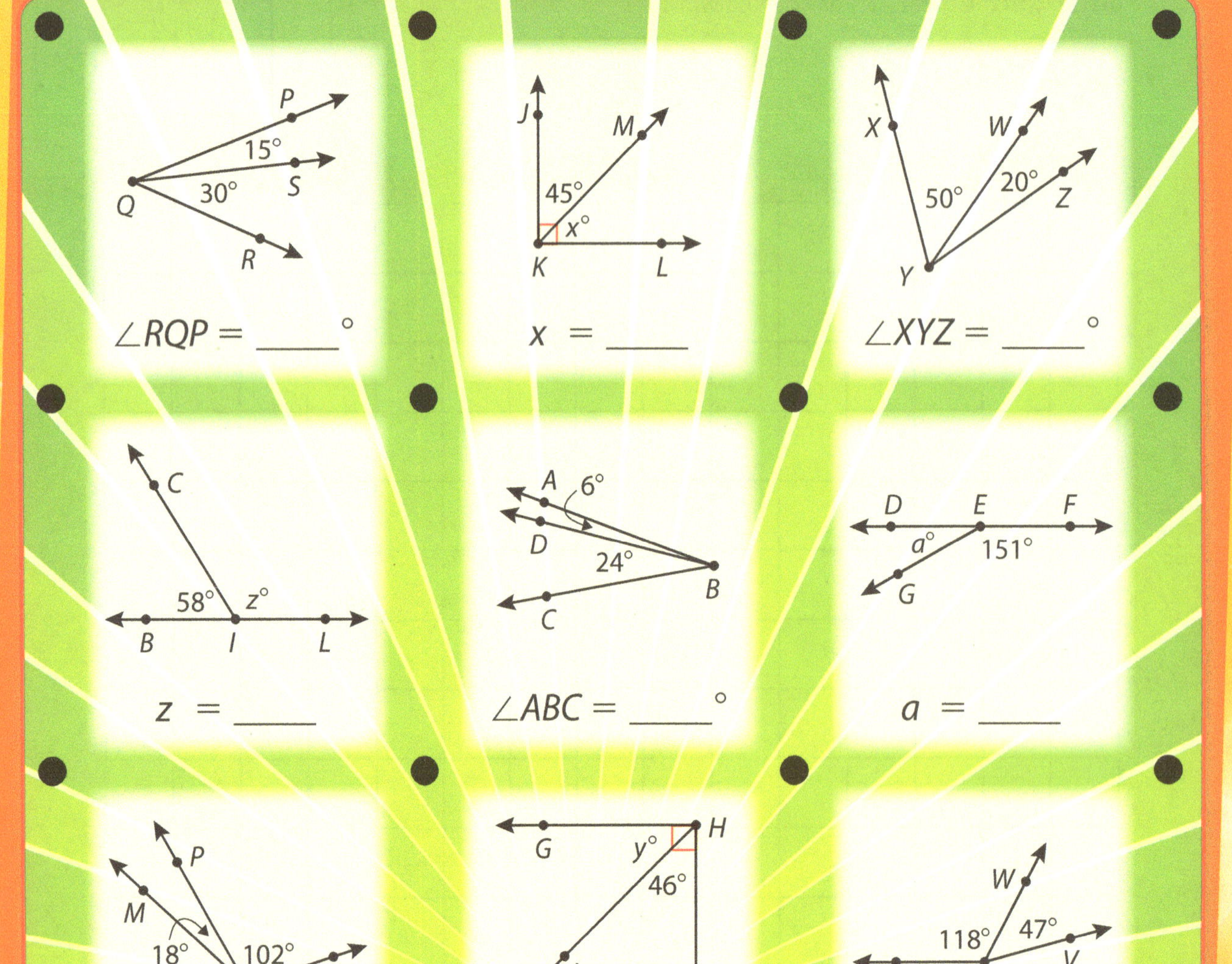

Copyright © Big Ideas Learning, LLC.
All rights reserved.

Pyramid Climb and Slide

Directions:

1. Players take turns spinning the spinner.
2. On your turn, move your counter to the next triangle that best matches your spin.
3. If you land at the bottom of a ladder, climb to the top of the ladder. If you land at the top of a slide, slide down to the bottom of the slide.
4. The first player to reach the top of the pyramid wins!

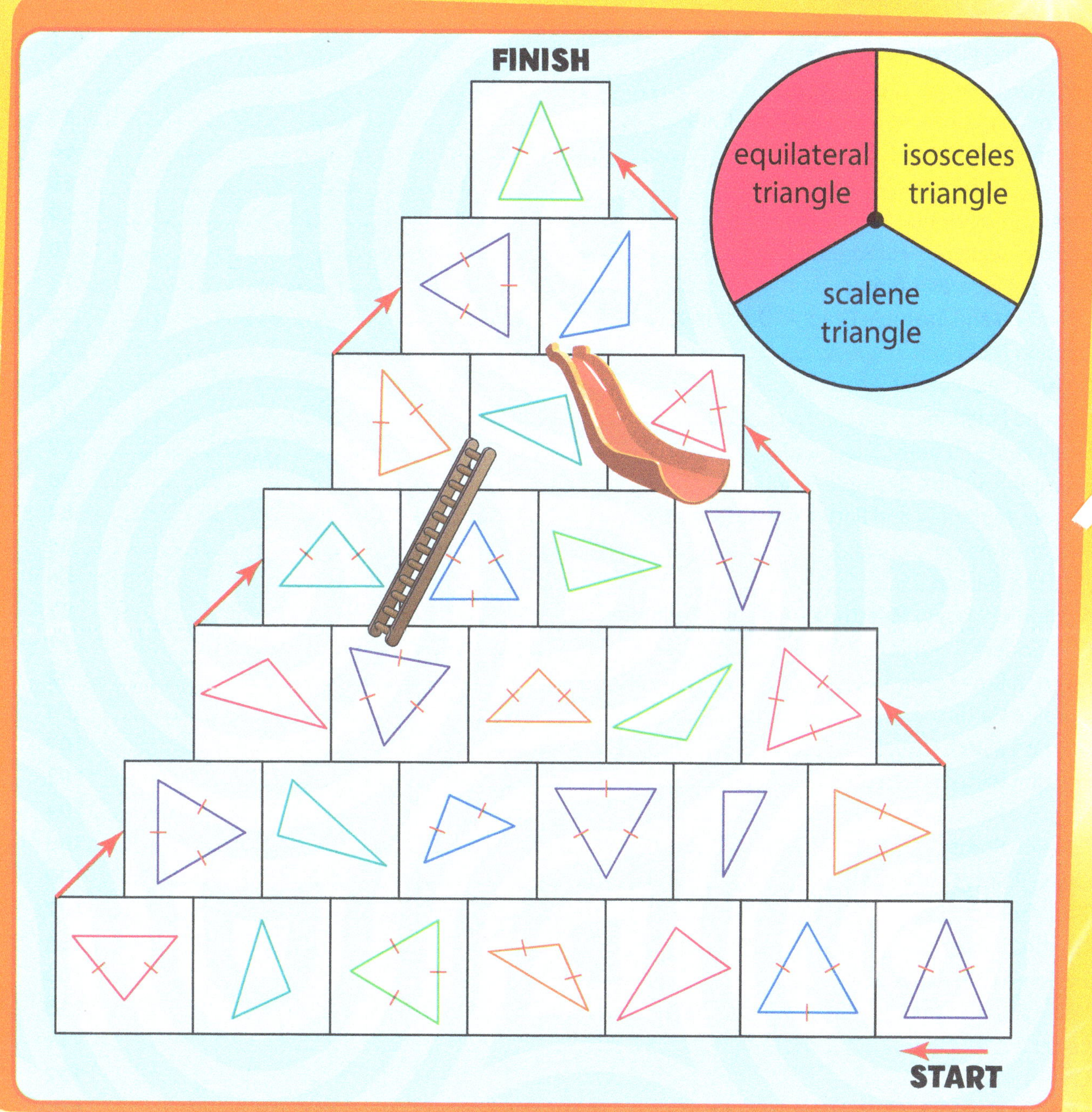

Copyright © Big Ideas Learning, LLC.
All rights reserved.

Blackline Masters

Copyright © Big Ideas Learning, LLC.
All rights reserved.

Blackline Masters (continued)

Copyright © Big Ideas Learning, LLC.
All rights reserved.

Name ______________________

Addition and Subtraction Word Cards

+ Addition +

combine	altogether
plus	increase
in all	both
add	join
sum	total

Copyright © Big Ideas Learning, LLC.
All rights reserved.

Name ______________________________

Addition and Subtraction Word Cards (continued)

— Subtraction —

how many more	left
subtract	decrease
remain	difference
minus	less than
fewer	take away

Copyright © Big Ideas Learning, LLC.
All rights reserved.

Name ______________________________

Angle Measurements Puzzle

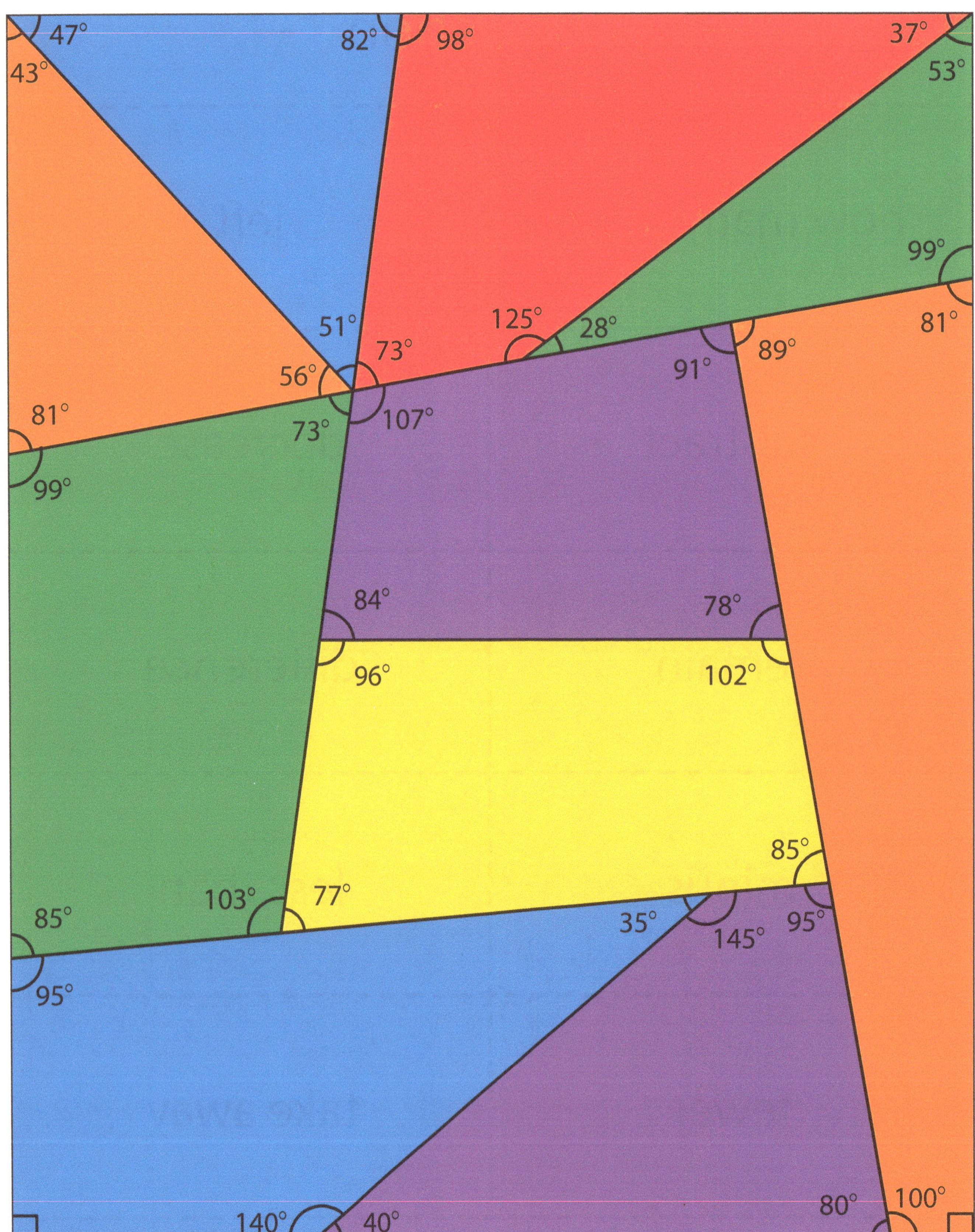

Copyright © Big Ideas Learning, LLC.
All rights reserved.

Area and Perimeter Flip and Spin

Name ______________________________

Largest Area | Smallest Perimeter
Smallest Area | Largest Perimeter

Round 1 Winner	
Round 2 Winner	
Round 3 Winner	
Round 4 Winner	
Round 5 Winner	
Round 6 Winner	

Name ______________________________

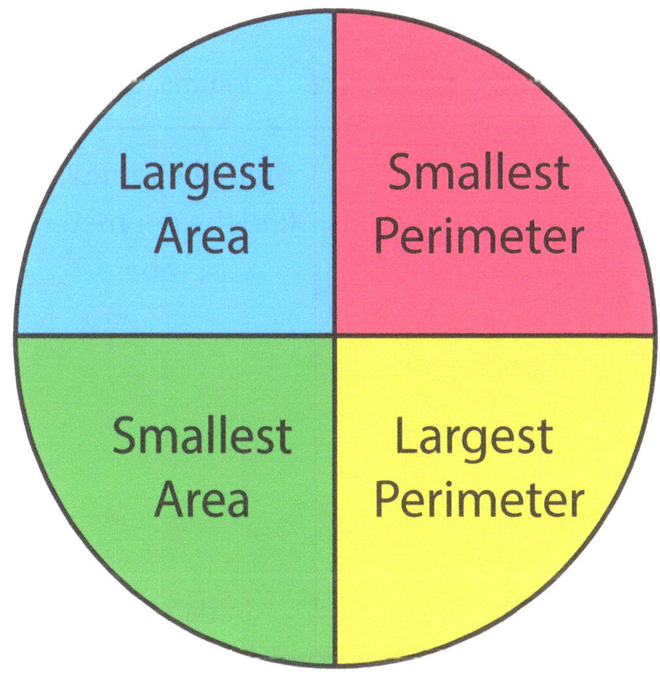

Round 1 Winner	
Round 2 Winner	
Round 3 Winner	
Round 4 Winner	
Round 5 Winner	
Round 6 Winner	

Copyright © Big Ideas Learning, LLC.
All rights reserved.

Name ______________________________

Area and Perimeter Search

Directions: Find a different classmate to solve, record, and initial each box.

State the formula to find the area of a rectangle. initials: _____	Find the perimeter of a rectangle that has a length of 14 meters and a width of 31 meters. initials: _____	State the difference between area and perimeter. initials: _____	Find the area of a rectangle that has a length of 56 feet and a width of 12 feet. initials: _____
State the type of unit all area measurements are labeled with. initials: _____	Find the unknown side length of a rectangle that has an area of 108 square yards and a width of 9 yards. initials: _____	State the formula to find the area of a square. initials: _____	Find the perimeter of a square with a side length of 15 inches. initials: _____
Find the unknown width of a rectangle that has a perimeter of 86 centimeters and a length of 23 centimeters. initials: _____	State the formula to find the perimeter of a rectangle. initials: _____	Find the unknown side length of a square that has an area of 144 square meters. initials: _____	State the formula to find the perimeter of a square. initials: _____

Copyright © Big Ideas Learning, LLC.
All rights reserved.

Blank Fraction Template

Name ______________________

Thirds

____ groups of $\frac{2}{3}$ = ____

Name ______________________

Fourths

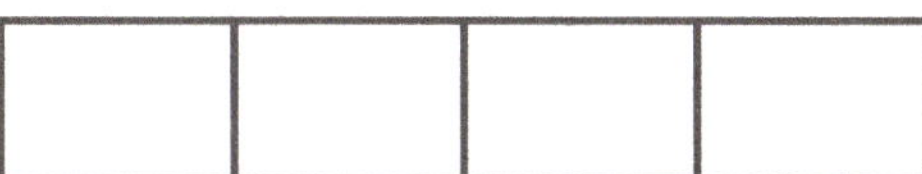

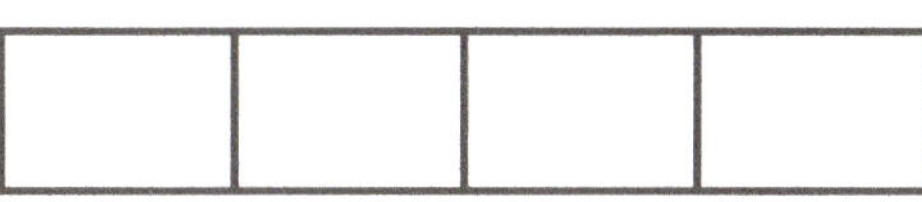

____ groups of $\frac{3}{4}$ = ____

Name ______________________

Fifths

____ groups of $\frac{4}{5}$ = ____

Name ______________________

Sixths

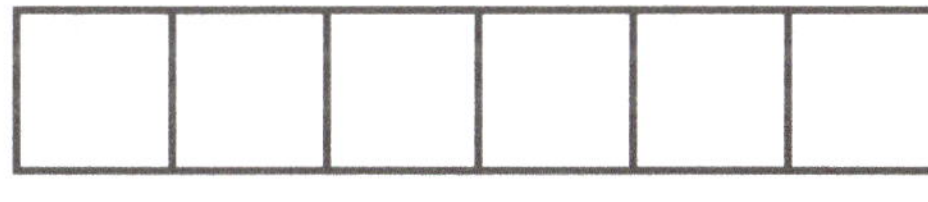

____ groups of $\frac{5}{6}$ = ____

Copyright © Big Ideas Learning, LLC.
All rights reserved.

Blank Sixths Template

Name ______________________

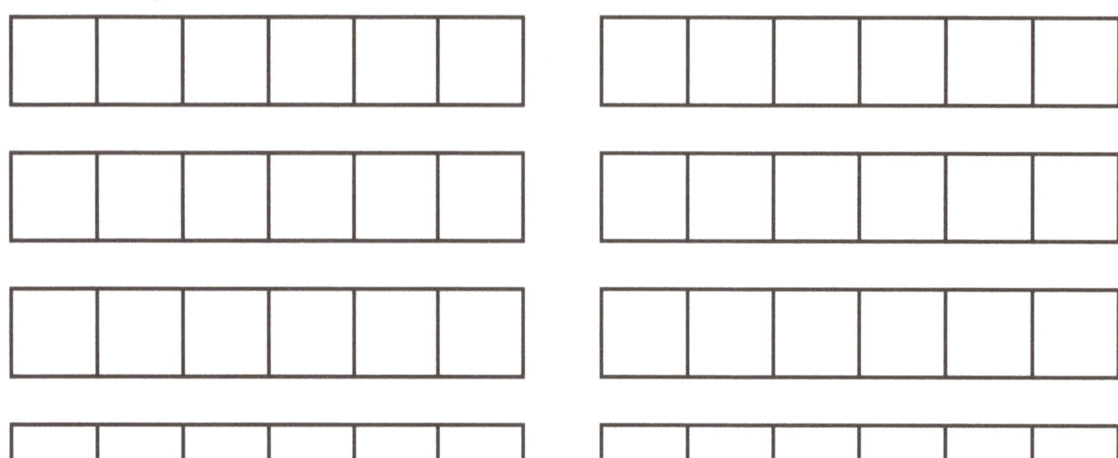

_____ groups of $\frac{2}{3}$ = $\frac{\square}{\square}$ or $\square\frac{\square}{\square}$

Name ______________________

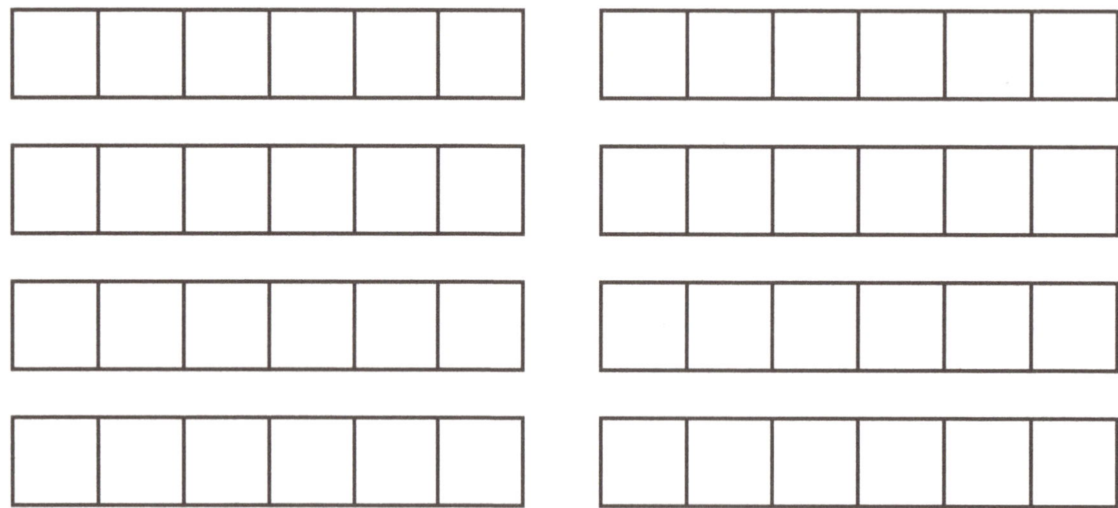

_____ groups of $\frac{2}{3}$ = $\frac{\square}{\square}$ or $\square\frac{\square}{\square}$

Copyright © Big Ideas Learning, LLC.
All rights reserved.

Name ______________________________

Captain Quotient's Treasure

Captain Quotient has buried his treasure. To keep it hidden, he has marked the map with decoy sites. To find the real treaure, solve the division equations and cross out the matching quotients on the map. The treasure is located at the site that is *not* crossed off!

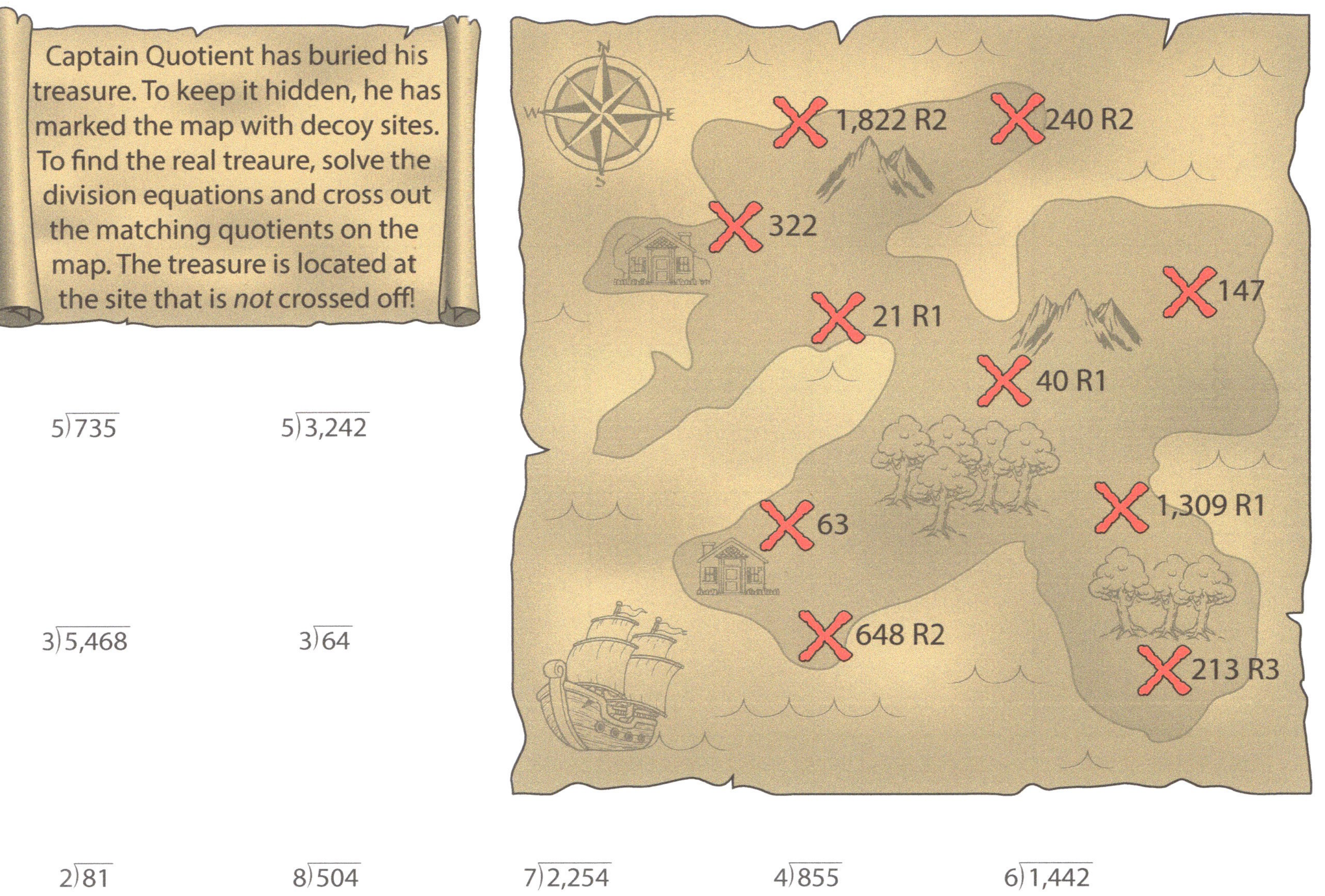

$5\overline{)735}$ $5\overline{)3{,}242}$

$3\overline{)5{,}468}$ $3\overline{)64}$

$2\overline{)81}$ $8\overline{)504}$ $7\overline{)2{,}254}$ $4\overline{)855}$ $6\overline{)1{,}442}$

Copyright © Big Ideas Learning, LLC.
All rights reserved.

Name ______________________________

Classifying Triangles Foldable

		Side Lengths		
	Key	Equilateral	Isosceles	Scalene
Angle Measures	Acute			
	Obtuse			
	Right			
	Equiangular			

Copyright © Big Ideas Learning, LLC.
All rights reserved.

Name ____________________

Comparing Place Value Game

Game	hundred thousands	ten thousands	thousands	hundreds	tens	ones	Points
1							
2							
3							
4							
5							
6							
7							
8							
9							
10							

Copyright © Big Ideas Learning, LLC.
All rights reserved.

Name ____________________

Concept Map Graphic Organizer

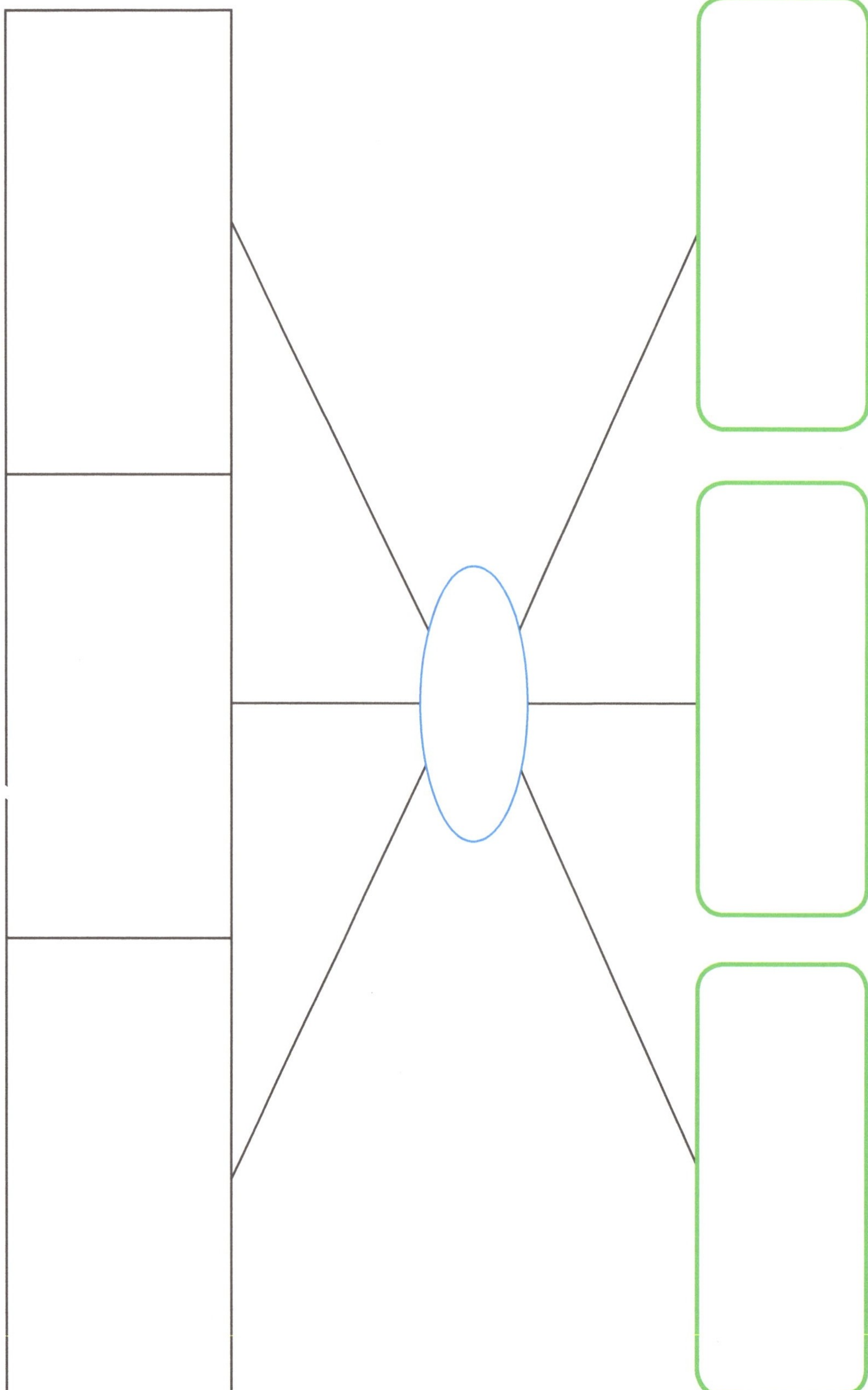

Copyright © Big Ideas Learning, LLC.
All rights reserved.

Name ______________________________

Customary Conversion Flip and Find Cards

7 ft	84 in.	5 yd	15 ft
3 mi	5,280 yd	9 lb	144 oz
4 T	8,000 lb	8 pt	16 c
2 qt	4 pt	6 gal	24 qt

Copyright © Big Ideas Learning, LLC.
All rights reserved.

Name ______________________________

Decimal Boss Cards

0.2	0.5	0.8
0.9	0.15	0.09
0.38	0.79	0.01
0.42	0.6	0.44

Copyright © Big Ideas Learning, LLC.
All rights reserved.

Name ______________________

Decimal Boss Cards (continued)

$\frac{1}{10}$	$\frac{3}{10}$	$\frac{4}{10}$
$\frac{7}{10}$	$\frac{28}{100}$	$\frac{51}{100}$
$\frac{4}{100}$	$\frac{63}{100}$	$\frac{32}{100}$
$\frac{84}{100}$	$\frac{17}{100}$	$\frac{98}{100}$

Copyright © Big Ideas Learning, LLC.
All rights reserved.

Name ______________________________

Decimal Place Value Mat (Hundredths)

Hundredths	
Tenths	
.	
Ones	
Tens	

Copyright © Big Ideas Learning, LLC.
All rights reserved.

Name ______________________

Decimal Place Value Mat (Tenths)

Tens	Ones	.	Tenths

Copyright © Big Ideas Learning, LLC.
All rights reserved.

Decimal Squares – Hundredths

Name ______________________

Name ______________________

Name ______________________

Name ______________________

Copyright © Big Ideas Learning, LLC.
All rights reserved.

Decimal Squares - Tenths

Name ______________________

Name ______________________

Name ______________________

Name ______________________

Copyright © Big Ideas Learning, LLC.
All rights reserved.

Name ___________________________

Definition and Example Graphic Organizer

Definition

Example

Example

Example

Copyright © Big Ideas Learning, LLC.
All rights reserved.

Name ___________________________

Division Fact Find

Directions:

1. Players take turns coloring a line of three numbers that make a division equation.
2. On your turn, find a set of three touching numbers, either in a row or in a column, that create a division equation.
3. The last player to color a division equation wins!

Game A

56	20	7	24	4	6
8	5	81	8	2	3
36	4	9	3	28	2
6	18	9	49	7	7
6	40	27	3	4	63
72	8	9	7	56	9
15	5	3	1	3	9
6	14	2	7	21	1
70	7	10	48	6	8

Game B

48	6	8	14	42	3
5	2	12	1	7	90
18	3	6	54	6	9
16	8	2	25	5	10
4	64	8	8	35	32
4	8	63	9	7	8
15	50	6	20	5	4
45	5	9	3	3	4
35	10	21	3	7	1

Copyright © Big Ideas Learning, LLC.
All rights reserved.

Name ___________________

Division Fact Puzzles

4	5	6
6	7	8
24	30	56

Copyright © Big Ideas Learning, LLC.
All rights reserved.

Name ______________________________

Division Fact Puzzles (continued)

2	3	4
5	6	6
10	12	36

Copyright © Big Ideas Learning, LLC.
All rights reserved.

Name ______________________

Division Fact Puzzles (continued)

2	3	3
6	7	9
14	18	27

Copyright © Big Ideas Learning, LLC.
All rights reserved.

Name ______________________

Domino Fractions

$\frac{4}{10}$ | $\frac{3}{5}$	$\frac{1}{3}$ | $\frac{2}{4}$
$\frac{2}{8}$ | $\frac{3}{4}$	$\frac{1}{2}$ | $\frac{2}{12}$
$\frac{6}{8}$ | $\frac{4}{5}$	$\frac{2}{3}$ | $\frac{2}{6}$
$\frac{1}{4}$ | $\frac{4}{6}$	$\frac{8}{10}$ | $\frac{2}{5}$
$\frac{2}{5}$ | $\frac{6}{8}$	$\frac{4}{6}$ | $\frac{3}{4}$

Copyright © Big Ideas Learning, LLC.
All rights reserved.

Name ______________________

Domino Fractions (continued)

$\frac{2}{8}$	$\frac{4}{5}$
$\frac{2}{6}$	$\frac{1}{4}$
$\frac{2}{10}$	$\frac{1}{6}$
$\frac{2}{3}$	$\frac{2}{4}$
$\frac{2}{12}$	$\frac{1}{3}$
$\frac{1}{5}$	$\frac{6}{10}$
$\frac{1}{4}$	$\frac{5}{6}$
$\frac{80}{100}$	$\frac{4}{24}$
$\frac{1}{6}$	$\frac{10}{12}$
$\frac{1}{5}$	$\frac{1}{4}$

Copyright © Big Ideas Learning, LLC.
All rights reserved.

Name ______________________________

Domino Fractions (continued)

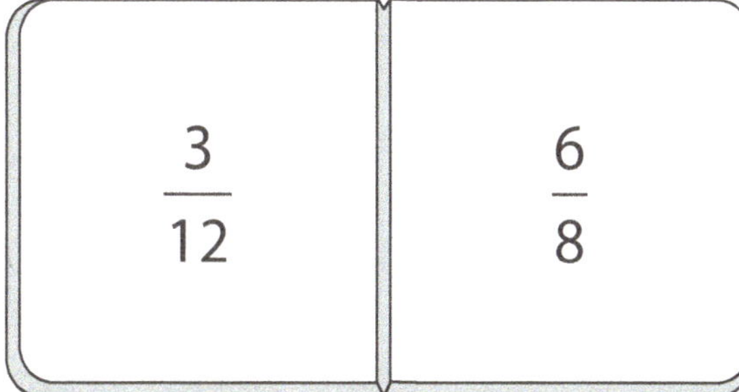

$\frac{4}{12}$ | $\frac{50}{100}$

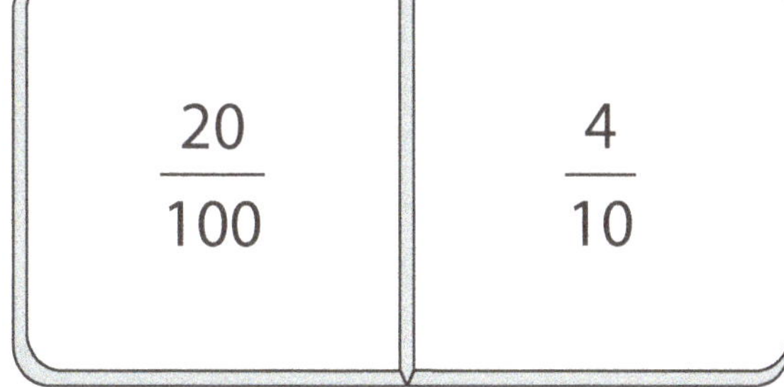

$\frac{2}{10}$ | $\frac{1}{4}$

$\frac{2}{5}$ | $\frac{60}{100}$

$\frac{3}{5}$ | $\frac{10}{100}$

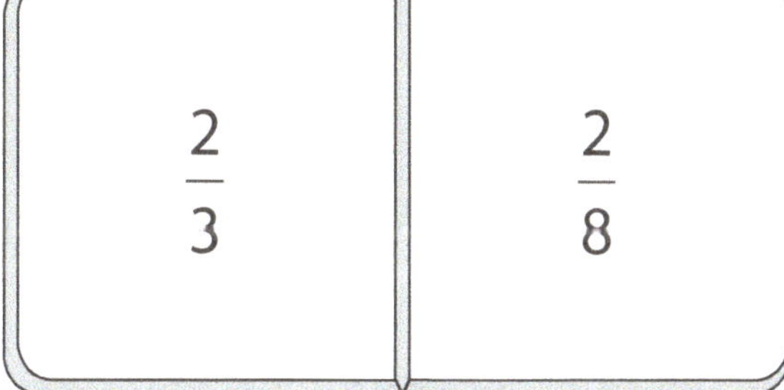

$\frac{1}{4}$ | $\frac{6}{8}$

$\frac{3}{5}$ | $\frac{8}{10}$

$\frac{2}{10}$ | $\frac{3}{4}$

Copyright © Big Ideas Learning, LLC.
All rights reserved.

Name ___________________________

Domino Fractions (continued)

$\frac{2}{5}$ | $\frac{6}{10}$	$\frac{4}{6}$ | $\frac{1}{3}$
$\frac{3}{5}$ | $\frac{8}{10}$	$\frac{4}{5}$ | $\frac{2}{5}$
$\frac{1}{4}$ | $\frac{3}{5}$	$\frac{6}{10}$ | $\frac{1}{6}$
$\frac{1}{5}$ | $\frac{4}{10}$	$\frac{1}{2}$ | $\frac{2}{10}$
$\frac{3}{6}$ | $\frac{2}{10}$	$\frac{1}{3}$ | $\frac{2}{12}$

Copyright © Big Ideas Learning, LLC.
All rights reserved.

Name ______________________________

Domino Fractions (continued)

$\frac{5}{6}$	$\frac{2}{6}$
$\frac{4}{10}$	$\frac{1}{5}$
$\frac{4}{5}$	$\frac{2}{12}$
$\frac{1}{6}$	$\frac{10}{12}$
$\frac{8}{12}$	$\frac{3}{9}$
$\frac{3}{4}$	$\frac{3}{12}$
$\frac{9}{12}$	$\frac{20}{100}$
$\frac{6}{9}$	$\frac{25}{100}$

Copyright © Big Ideas Learning, LLC.
All rights reserved.

Name ___________________________

Equivalent Fractions

One Whole											

$\frac{1}{2}$	$\frac{1}{2}$

$\frac{1}{3}$	$\frac{1}{3}$	$\frac{1}{3}$

$\frac{1}{4}$	$\frac{1}{4}$	$\frac{1}{4}$	$\frac{1}{4}$

$\frac{1}{5}$	$\frac{1}{5}$	$\frac{1}{5}$	$\frac{1}{5}$	$\frac{1}{5}$

$\frac{1}{6}$	$\frac{1}{6}$	$\frac{1}{6}$	$\frac{1}{6}$	$\frac{1}{6}$	$\frac{1}{6}$

$\frac{1}{8}$	$\frac{1}{8}$	$\frac{1}{8}$	$\frac{1}{8}$	$\frac{1}{8}$	$\frac{1}{8}$	$\frac{1}{8}$	$\frac{1}{8}$

$\frac{1}{10}$	$\frac{1}{10}$	$\frac{1}{10}$	$\frac{1}{10}$	$\frac{1}{10}$	$\frac{1}{10}$	$\frac{1}{10}$	$\frac{1}{10}$	$\frac{1}{10}$	$\frac{1}{10}$

$\frac{1}{12}$	$\frac{1}{12}$	$\frac{1}{12}$	$\frac{1}{12}$	$\frac{1}{12}$	$\frac{1}{12}$	$\frac{1}{12}$	$\frac{1}{12}$	$\frac{1}{12}$	$\frac{1}{12}$	$\frac{1}{12}$	$\frac{1}{12}$

Copyright © Big Ideas Learning, LLC.
All rights reserved.

Name ______________________

Example and Non-Example Graphic Organizer

Non-Example	
Example	

Copyright © Big Ideas Learning, LLC.
All rights reserved.

Name ______________________________

Factors, Multiples, and Patterns Assessment

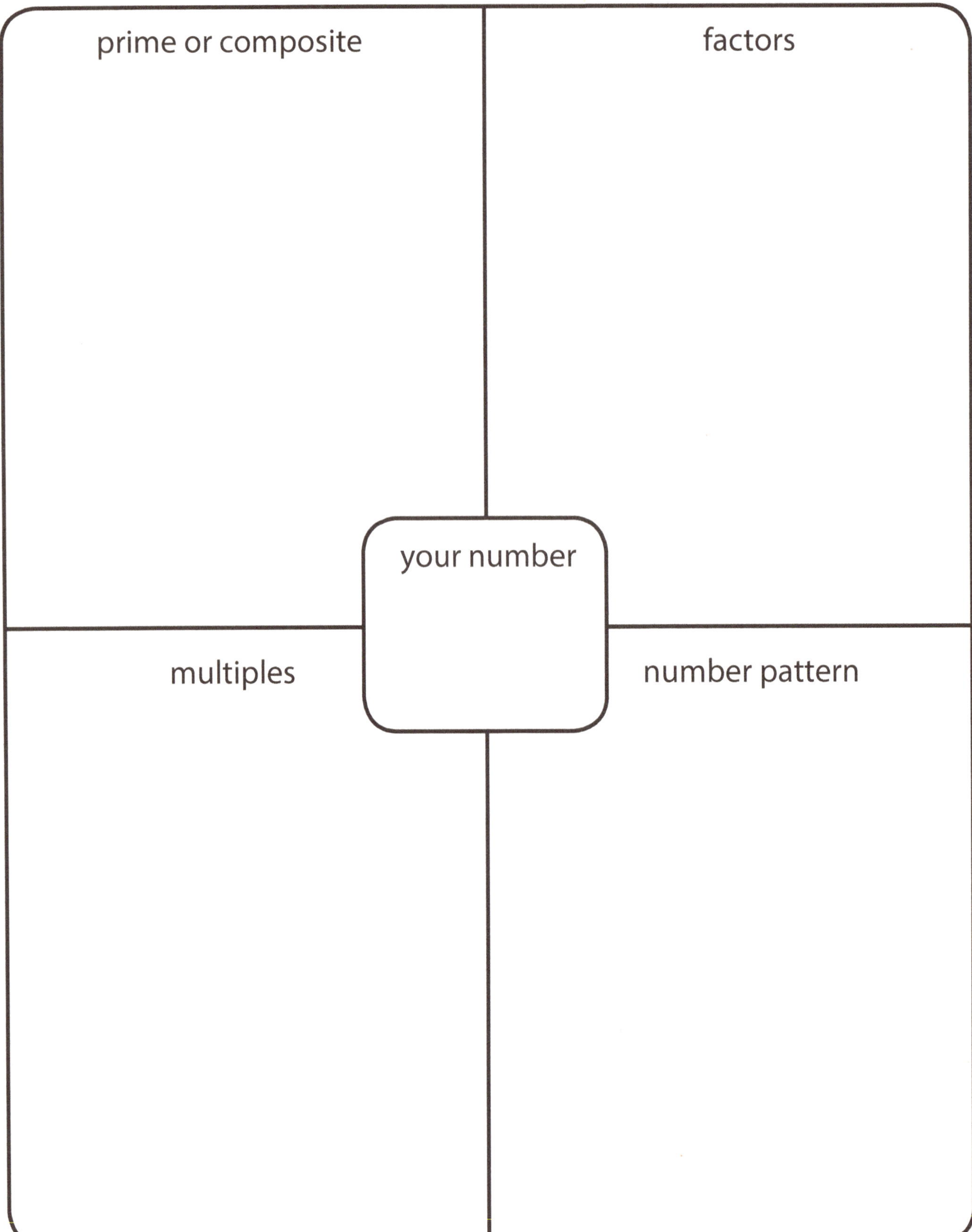

Copyright © Big Ideas Learning, LLC.
All rights reserved.

Name ______________________________

Find the Answer

What bird never has to go to the barber?

E	A	L
The Queen Alexandra's birdwing wingspan is 28 centimeters long. How many millimeters is its wingspan? 28 cm = _____ mm	An emu egg has a mass of $\frac{1}{2}$ kilogram. What is the mass in grams? $\frac{1}{2}$ kg = _____ g	A kangaroo can jump 10 yards. How many inches can the kangaroo jump? 10 yd = _____ in.
L	**A**	**B**
A hive of 50,000 bees weighs 12 pounds. How many ounces does the hive weigh? 12 lb = _____ oz	A giraffe's neck is 2 yards. How many inches is its neck? 2 yd = _____ in.	An elephant can hold up to 14 liters of water in its trunk. How many milliliters can it hold? 14 L = _____ mL
G	**E**	**D**
The American White Pelican can hold 3 gallons of water in its pouch. How many pints can it hold? 3 gal = _____ pt	An elephant weighs 6 tons. How many pounds does the elephant weigh? 6 T = _____ lb	The average lifespan of a Labrador Retriever is 12 years. How many weeks are in 12 years? 12 yr = _____ wk

A
A resting sea turtle can stay underwater for 7 hours. How many seconds can it stay underwater? 7 h = _____ sec

_____   _____ _____ _____ _____
500   14,000 25,200 360 624

_____ _____ _____ _____ _____!
280 72 24 192 12,000

Copyright © Big Ideas Learning, LLC.
All rights reserved.

Name ______________________

Find the Remainder

Directions:

1. Take a handful of base ten blocks. Record the number of base ten blocks under "Dividend."
2. Roll the dice. Record the number rolled under "Divisor."
3. Divide your base ten blocks by the number rolled on the dice.
4. Record the quotient and remainder.

Dividend (number of base ten blocks)	Divisor (number on die)	Quotient (number of groups)	Remainder (number left over)

Copyright © Big Ideas Learning, LLC.
All rights reserved.

Name ______________________

Finding Unknown Measures – Area and Perimeter

Area = 25 square inches

5 in.

a in.

a = ____ inches

Perimeter = 20 inches

5 in.

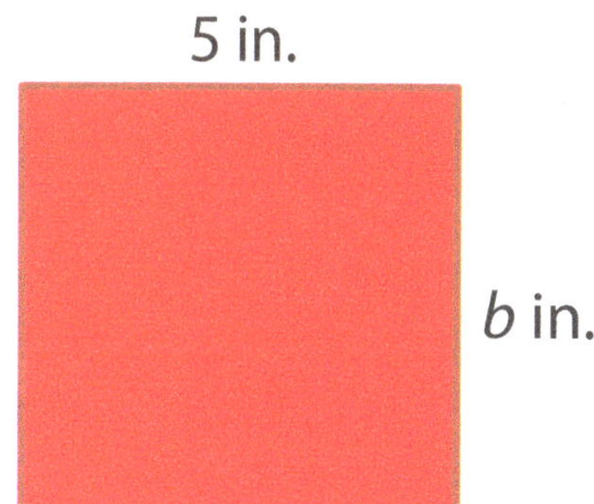

b in.

b = ____ inches

Area = 15 square inches

c in.

3 in.

c = ____ inches

Perimeter = 16 inches

f in.

3 in.

f = ____ inches

Copyright © Big Ideas Learning, LLC.
All rights reserved.

Name ______________________________

Finding Unknown Measures – Area and Perimeter (continued)

Area = 121 square feet

11 ft

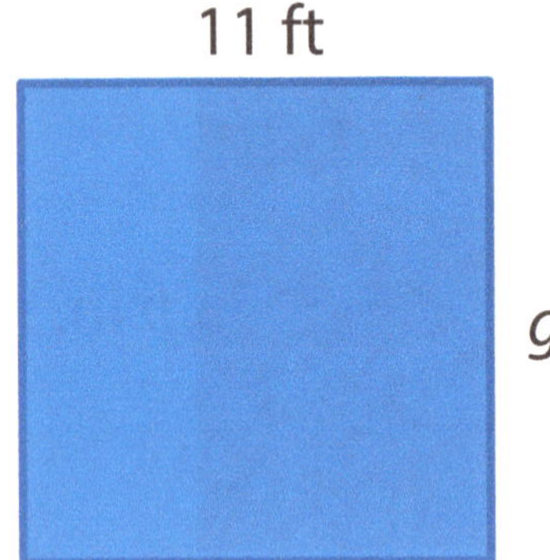

g ft

g = ____ feet

Perimeter = 44 feet

11 ft

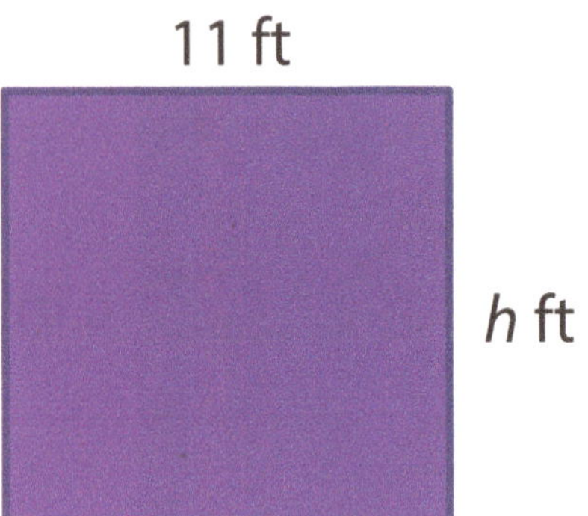

h ft

h = ____ feet

Area = 48 square centimeters

8 cm

j cm

j = ____ centimeters

Perimeter = 28 centimeters

8 cm

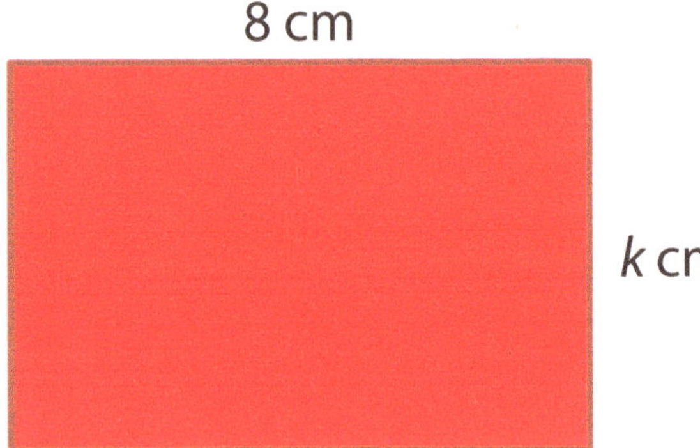

k cm

k = ____ centimeters

Copyright © Big Ideas Learning, LLC.
All rights reserved.

Name ______________________

Finding Unknown Measures – Area and Perimeter (continued)

Area = 49 square feet

m = ____ feet

Perimeter = 28 feet

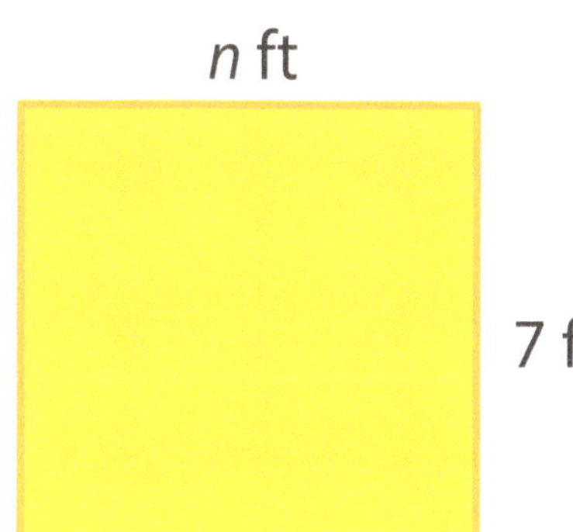

n = ____ feet

Area = $40\frac{1}{2}$ square inches

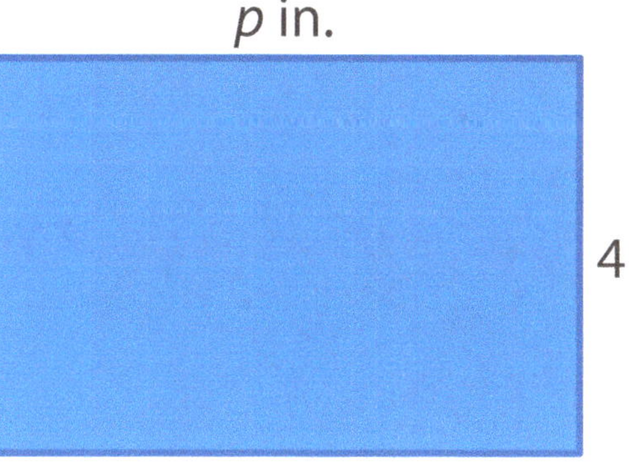

p = ____ inches

Perimeter = 27 inches

q = ____ inches

Copyright © Big Ideas Learning, LLC.
All rights reserved.

Name ______________________

Finding Unknown Measures – Area and Perimeter (continued)

Area = 120 square meters

s m

8 m

s = ____ meters

Perimeter = 46 meters

u m

8 m

u = ____ meters

Area = 132 square yards

13 yd

w yd

w = ____ yards

Perimeter = 46 yards

13 yd

z yd

z = ____ yards

Copyright © Big Ideas Learning, LLC.
All rights reserved.

Name ______________________________

Four Square Graphic Organizer

Copyright © Big Ideas Learning, LLC.
All rights reserved.

Name ______________________

Fraction Boss Cards

$\frac{1}{2}$	$\frac{2}{2}$	$\frac{1}{3}$
$\frac{2}{3}$	$\frac{3}{3}$	$\frac{1}{4}$
$\frac{2}{4}$	$\frac{3}{4}$	$\frac{4}{4}$

Copyright © Big Ideas Learning, LLC.
All rights reserved.

Name ____________________

Fraction Boss Cards (continued)

$\frac{1}{5}$	$\frac{4}{5}$	$\frac{5}{5}$
$\frac{1}{6}$	$\frac{3}{6}$	$\frac{5}{6}$
$\frac{6}{6}$	$\frac{1}{8}$	$\frac{2}{8}$

Copyright © Big Ideas Learning, LLC.
All rights reserved.

Name ______________________

Fraction Boss Cards (continued)

$\frac{4}{8}$	$\frac{7}{8}$	$\frac{8}{8}$
$\frac{1}{10}$	$\frac{2}{10}$	$\frac{5}{10}$
$\frac{8}{10}$	$\frac{9}{10}$	$\frac{10}{10}$

Copyright © Big Ideas Learning, LLC.
All rights reserved.

Name ___________________________

Fraction Boss Cards (continued)

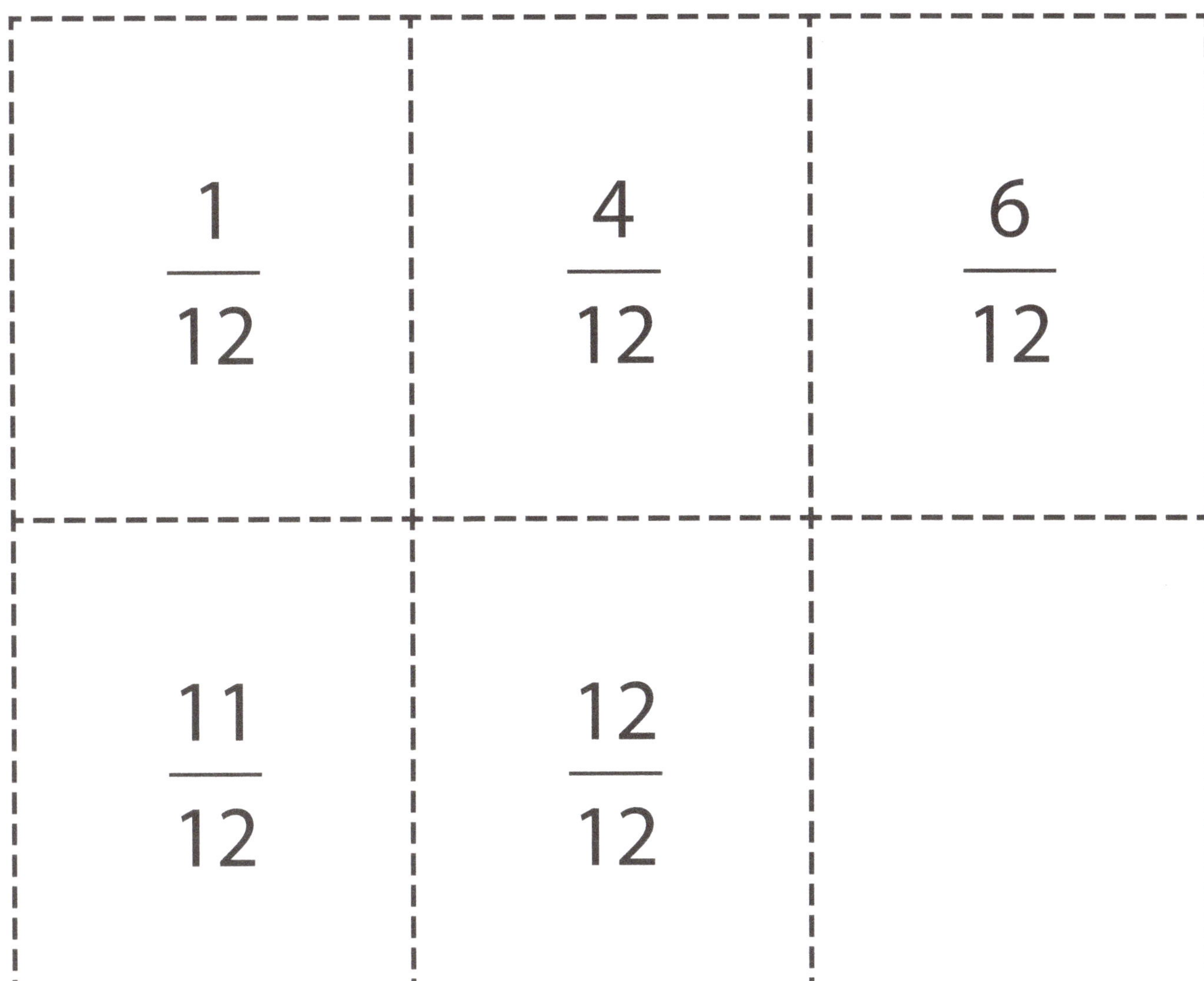

Copyright © Big Ideas Learning, LLC.
All rights reserved.

Name ______________________

Fraction Cards

$\frac{1}{1}$	$\frac{1}{2}$	$\frac{2}{2}$
$\frac{1}{3}$	$\frac{2}{3}$	$\frac{3}{3}$
$\frac{1}{4}$	$\frac{2}{4}$	$\frac{3}{4}$

Copyright © Big Ideas Learning, LLC.
All rights reserved.

Name ______________________

Fraction Cards (continued)

$\frac{4}{4}$	$\frac{1}{5}$	$\frac{2}{5}$
$\frac{3}{5}$	$\frac{4}{5}$	$\frac{5}{5}$
$\frac{1}{6}$	$\frac{2}{6}$	$\frac{3}{6}$

Copyright © Big Ideas Learning, LLC.
All rights reserved.

Name ______________________

Fraction Cards (continued)

$\frac{4}{6}$	$\frac{5}{6}$	$\frac{6}{6}$
$\frac{1}{8}$	$\frac{2}{8}$	$\frac{3}{8}$
$\frac{4}{8}$	$\frac{5}{8}$	$\frac{6}{8}$

Copyright © Big Ideas Learning, LLC.
All rights reserved.

Name ______________________

Fraction Cards (continued)

$\frac{7}{8}$	$\frac{8}{8}$	$\frac{1}{10}$
$\frac{2}{10}$	$\frac{3}{10}$	$\frac{4}{10}$
$\frac{5}{10}$	$\frac{6}{10}$	$\frac{7}{10}$

Copyright © Big Ideas Learning, LLC.
All rights reserved.

Name ______________________

Fraction Cards (continued)

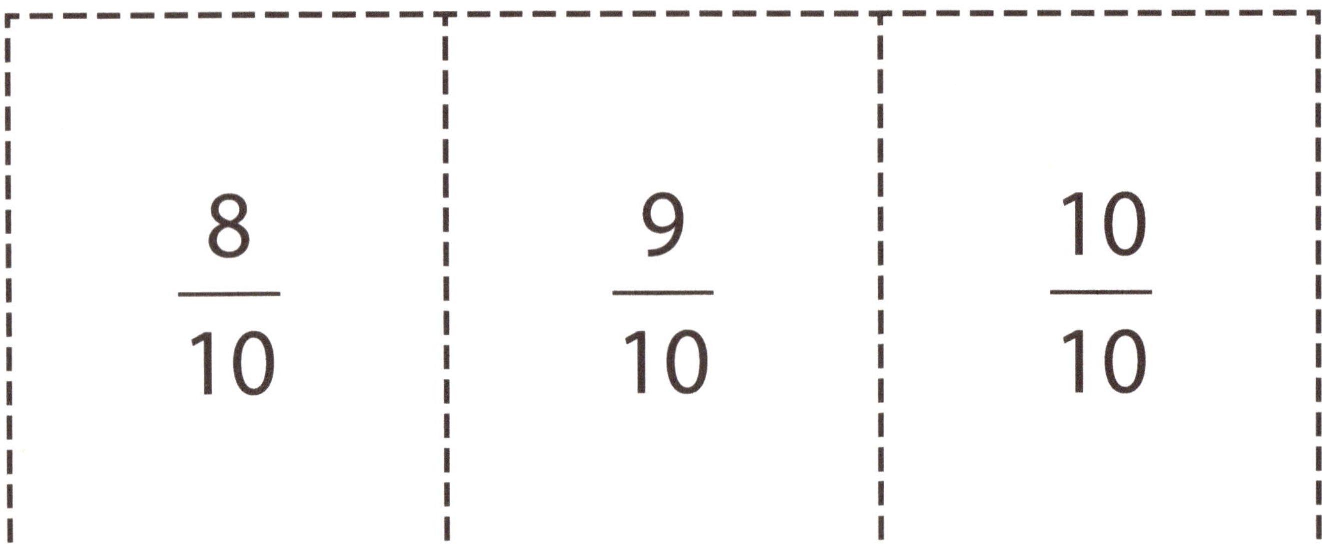

Copyright © Big Ideas Learning, LLC.
All rights reserved.

Name ____________________

Fraction Match Up

$7 \times \frac{1}{2}$	$2 \times \frac{2}{2}$	$6 \times \frac{1}{3}$
$2 \times \frac{2}{3}$	$5 \times \frac{3}{3}$	$7 \times \frac{1}{4}$
$2 \times \frac{2}{6}$	$1 \times \frac{3}{8}$	$3 \times \frac{1}{6}$

Copyright © Big Ideas Learning, LLC.
All rights reserved.

Name ____________________

Fraction Match Up (continued)

$\frac{1}{2}$	$\frac{1}{2}$
$\frac{1}{2}$	$\frac{1}{2}$
$\frac{1}{2}$	$\frac{1}{2}$
$\frac{1}{2}$	$\frac{1}{2}$
$\frac{1}{2}$	$\frac{1}{2}$
$\frac{1}{2}$	$\frac{1}{2}$
$\frac{1}{2}$	$\frac{1}{2}$

$\frac{1}{2}$	$\frac{1}{2}$
$\frac{1}{2}$	$\frac{1}{2}$

$\frac{1}{3}$	$\frac{1}{3}$	$\frac{1}{3}$
$\frac{1}{3}$	$\frac{1}{3}$	$\frac{1}{3}$
$\frac{1}{3}$	$\frac{1}{3}$	$\frac{1}{3}$
$\frac{1}{3}$	$\frac{1}{3}$	$\frac{1}{3}$
$\frac{1}{3}$	$\frac{1}{3}$	$\frac{1}{3}$
$\frac{1}{3}$	$\frac{1}{3}$	$\frac{1}{3}$

$\frac{1}{3}$	$\frac{1}{3}$	$\frac{1}{3}$
$\frac{1}{3}$	$\frac{1}{3}$	$\frac{1}{3}$

$\frac{1}{3}$	$\frac{1}{3}$	$\frac{1}{3}$
$\frac{1}{3}$	$\frac{1}{3}$	$\frac{1}{3}$
$\frac{1}{3}$	$\frac{1}{3}$	$\frac{1}{3}$
$\frac{1}{3}$	$\frac{1}{3}$	$\frac{1}{3}$
$\frac{1}{3}$	$\frac{1}{3}$	$\frac{1}{3}$

$\frac{1}{4}$	$\frac{1}{4}$	$\frac{1}{4}$	$\frac{1}{4}$
$\frac{1}{4}$	$\frac{1}{4}$	$\frac{1}{4}$	$\frac{1}{4}$
$\frac{1}{4}$	$\frac{1}{4}$	$\frac{1}{4}$	$\frac{1}{4}$
$\frac{1}{4}$	$\frac{1}{4}$	$\frac{1}{4}$	$\frac{1}{4}$
$\frac{1}{4}$	$\frac{1}{4}$	$\frac{1}{4}$	$\frac{1}{4}$
$\frac{1}{4}$	$\frac{1}{4}$	$\frac{1}{4}$	$\frac{1}{4}$
$\frac{1}{4}$	$\frac{1}{4}$	$\frac{1}{4}$	$\frac{1}{4}$

$\frac{1}{6}$	$\frac{1}{6}$	$\frac{1}{6}$	$\frac{1}{6}$	$\frac{1}{6}$	$\frac{1}{6}$
$\frac{1}{6}$	$\frac{1}{6}$	$\frac{1}{6}$	$\frac{1}{6}$	$\frac{1}{6}$	$\frac{1}{6}$

$\frac{1}{8}$	$\frac{1}{8}$	$\frac{1}{8}$	$\frac{1}{8}$	$\frac{1}{8}$	$\frac{1}{8}$	$\frac{1}{8}$	$\frac{1}{8}$

$\frac{1}{6}$	$\frac{1}{6}$	$\frac{1}{6}$	$\frac{1}{6}$	$\frac{1}{6}$	$\frac{1}{6}$
$\frac{1}{6}$	$\frac{1}{6}$	$\frac{1}{6}$	$\frac{1}{6}$	$\frac{1}{6}$	$\frac{1}{6}$
$\frac{1}{6}$	$\frac{1}{6}$	$\frac{1}{6}$	$\frac{1}{6}$	$\frac{1}{6}$	$\frac{1}{6}$

Copyright © Big Ideas Learning, LLC.
All rights reserved.

Name ______________________________

Fraction Pattern

Required Fraction Colors

red $= \frac{20}{50}$

blue $= \frac{4}{25}$

orange $= \frac{1}{4}$

purple $= \frac{6}{12}$

green $= \frac{10}{32}$

pink $= \frac{3}{4}$

Copyright © Big Ideas Learning, LLC.
All rights reserved.

Name ______________________________

Fraction Plot Cards

$\frac{3}{8}$	$\frac{5}{8}$	$\frac{7}{8}$
$\frac{3}{8}$	$\frac{5}{8}$	$\frac{7}{8}$
$\frac{3}{8}$	$\frac{5}{8}$	1
$\frac{4}{8}$	$\frac{5}{8}$	1
$\frac{5}{8}$	$\frac{6}{8}$	1

Copyright © Big Ideas Learning, LLC.
All rights reserved.

Fraction Strips

Name ____________________

1

$\frac{1}{2}$	$\frac{1}{2}$

$\frac{1}{3}$	$\frac{1}{3}$	$\frac{1}{3}$

$\frac{1}{4}$	$\frac{1}{4}$	$\frac{1}{4}$	$\frac{1}{4}$

$\frac{1}{5}$	$\frac{1}{5}$	$\frac{1}{5}$	$\frac{1}{5}$	$\frac{1}{5}$

$\frac{1}{6}$	$\frac{1}{6}$	$\frac{1}{6}$	$\frac{1}{6}$	$\frac{1}{6}$	$\frac{1}{6}$

$\frac{1}{8}$	$\frac{1}{8}$	$\frac{1}{8}$	$\frac{1}{8}$	$\frac{1}{8}$	$\frac{1}{8}$	$\frac{1}{8}$	$\frac{1}{8}$

$\frac{1}{10}$	$\frac{1}{10}$	$\frac{1}{10}$	$\frac{1}{10}$	$\frac{1}{10}$	$\frac{1}{10}$	$\frac{1}{10}$	$\frac{1}{10}$	$\frac{1}{10}$	$\frac{1}{10}$

$\frac{1}{12}$	$\frac{1}{12}$	$\frac{1}{12}$	$\frac{1}{12}$	$\frac{1}{12}$	$\frac{1}{12}$	$\frac{1}{12}$	$\frac{1}{12}$	$\frac{1}{12}$	$\frac{1}{12}$	$\frac{1}{12}$	$\frac{1}{12}$

Name ____________________

1

$\frac{1}{2}$	$\frac{1}{2}$

$\frac{1}{3}$	$\frac{1}{3}$	$\frac{1}{3}$

$\frac{1}{4}$	$\frac{1}{4}$	$\frac{1}{4}$	$\frac{1}{4}$

$\frac{1}{5}$	$\frac{1}{5}$	$\frac{1}{5}$	$\frac{1}{5}$	$\frac{1}{5}$

$\frac{1}{6}$	$\frac{1}{6}$	$\frac{1}{6}$	$\frac{1}{6}$	$\frac{1}{6}$	$\frac{1}{6}$

$\frac{1}{8}$	$\frac{1}{8}$	$\frac{1}{8}$	$\frac{1}{8}$	$\frac{1}{8}$	$\frac{1}{8}$	$\frac{1}{8}$	$\frac{1}{8}$

$\frac{1}{10}$	$\frac{1}{10}$	$\frac{1}{10}$	$\frac{1}{10}$	$\frac{1}{10}$	$\frac{1}{10}$	$\frac{1}{10}$	$\frac{1}{10}$	$\frac{1}{10}$	$\frac{1}{10}$

$\frac{1}{12}$	$\frac{1}{12}$	$\frac{1}{12}$	$\frac{1}{12}$	$\frac{1}{12}$	$\frac{1}{12}$	$\frac{1}{12}$	$\frac{1}{12}$	$\frac{1}{12}$	$\frac{1}{12}$	$\frac{1}{12}$	$\frac{1}{12}$

Copyright © Big Ideas Learning, LLC.
All rights reserved.

Name ____________________

Game Points Challenge

Game Points Challenge

Directions: You are playing your favorite video game. Start at the first event and add or subtract the points. Each event builds on the event before it. In the end, there is only one correct answer.

1: You start on your journey to defeat the Master Giant with 0 points. Within seconds of starting the game, you find a hidden skeleton key with **8,281 points**. You are off to a good start. Record the amount of points you have.

2: As you walk along the trail, you find a total of 100 gold coins. The coins add **12,300 points** to your score.

3: A few moments later, a fairy comes up behind you and steals 35 coins! Your score decreases by **5,167 points.**

4: You want to cross the bridge into the Master Giant's city and will need to battle a troll in order to cross. You buy more strength, which costs **3,804 points**.

5: You defeated the troll and gained **28,475 points!** Good job! Now you can cross the bridge.

6: You find the castle but run into dragons before heading into the castle. The dragons burn your shield. You will need to purchase another one that costs **15,074 points.**

7: You finally make it to the top of the castle and use the skeleton key to open the door to the finish line. You earn **3,642 points** and celebrate.

8: You finished Level 1 by jumping on a trampoline and making it to the sky in record time. Your score increases by **21,385 points.**

9: While battling the Master Giant, he jumped on you, and you have to restart the battle. **16,372 points** were taken away from your score.

10: You defeated the Master Giant! Great job! **53,861 points** were added to your score.

How many points do you end up with?

Copyright © Big Ideas Learning, LLC.
All rights reserved.

Name ______________________________

Grid Paper

Copyright © Big Ideas Learning, LLC.
All rights reserved.

Name ______________________

Hundred Chart

1	2	3	4	5	6	7	8	9	10
11	12	13	14	15	16	17	18	19	20
21	22	23	24	25	26	27	28	29	30
31	32	33	34	35	36	37	38	39	40
41	42	43	44	45	46	47	48	49	50
51	52	53	54	55	56	57	58	59	60
61	62	63	64	65	66	67	68	69	70
71	72	73	74	75	76	77	78	79	80
81	82	83	84	85	86	87	88	89	90
91	92	93	94	95	96	97	98	99	100

Copyright © Big Ideas Learning, LLC.
All rights reserved.

Name ______________________________

Hundred Grid Paper

Copyright © Big Ideas Learning, LLC.
All rights reserved.

Name ____________________

I Won Assessment

You won 10,000 + 7,000 + 700 + 50 + 6 dollars!

Directions: Write the cost of each item in standard form on the price tag. Compare the price of each item to the amount won. Circle the item you can purchase without spending extra money. Then complete the check by writing the amount of your prize in standard form and word form on the check.

Pool Cost:

10,000 + 7,000 + 900 + 60 + 7 dollars

Ticket Cost:

10,000 + 7,000 + 600 + 20 + 5 dollars

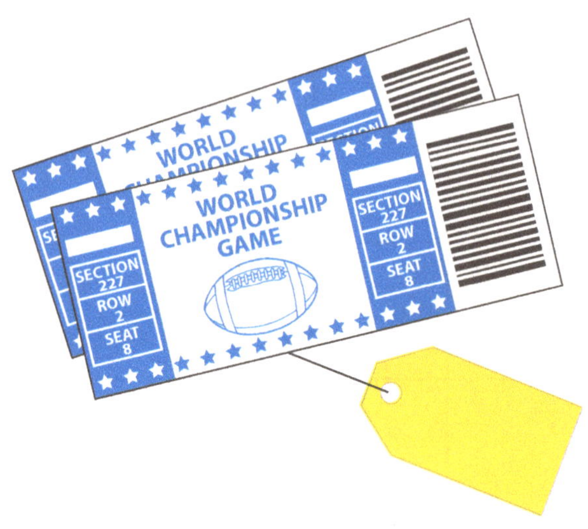

__________ ◯ __________

(Amount Won) (Pool Cost)

__________ ◯ __________

(Amount Won) (Ticket Cost)

0000

__________ DATE

PAY TO THE ORDER OF *Jackpot Prizes* $ [   ] (standard form)

(word form) ______________________________ DOLLARS

MEMO *Winning item* __________ AUTHORIZED SIGNATURE

123456789 09 02 12346694566 0003

Copyright © Big Ideas Learning, LLC.
All rights reserved.

Letter X

Name ______________________________

Name ______________________________

Copyright © Big Ideas Learning, LLC.
All rights reserved.

Name ______________________

Line Plot

____

____

Name ______________________

____

____

Copyright © Big Ideas Learning, LLC.
All rights reserved.

Name ______________________________

Line Plot Data Cards

$1\frac{3}{4}$	$2\frac{1}{2}$	$3\frac{1}{4}$
$1\frac{3}{4}$	$2\frac{1}{2}$	$3\frac{1}{4}$
2	$2\frac{3}{4}$	$2\frac{1}{2}$
$2\frac{1}{4}$	$2\frac{3}{4}$	$1\frac{3}{4}$
$2\frac{1}{2}$	3	$2\frac{3}{4}$

Copyright © Big Ideas Learning, LLC.
All rights reserved.

Name ______________________________

Make a Whole

Directions: Roll a die and move the indicated number of spaces. Write the fraction you landed on as an addend in an addition equation with 1 as the sum. Solve for the missing addend. The first player to get back to Newton wins!

	$\frac{2}{6}$	$\frac{1}{4}$	$\frac{3}{8}$	$\frac{1}{2}$	$\frac{2}{3}$	$\frac{4}{6}$	$\frac{2}{8}$
$\frac{6}{10}$							$\frac{1}{2}$
$\frac{1}{12}$	$\frac{8}{12}$	$\frac{5}{10}$		$\frac{3}{12}$	$\frac{1}{10}$	$\frac{2}{5}$	$\frac{2}{4}$
		$\frac{4}{5}$		$\frac{5}{8}$			
		$\frac{4}{12}$		$\frac{1}{3}$	$\frac{1}{6}$	$\frac{1}{2}$	$\frac{4}{10}$
		$\frac{5}{6}$					$\frac{3}{5}$
$\frac{2}{12}$	$\frac{1}{5}$	$\frac{7}{10}$					$\frac{1}{8}$
$\frac{4}{8}$							$\frac{7}{12}$
$\frac{3}{6}$	$\frac{4}{5}$	$\frac{2}{10}$	$\frac{9}{12}$	$\frac{6}{8}$	$\frac{7}{12}$	$\frac{3}{4}$	$\frac{3}{10}$

Copyright © Big Ideas Learning, LLC.
All rights reserved.

Name ______________________________

Match Fractions to a Mixed Number Flip and Find

$4\frac{1}{2}$	$3\frac{1}{3}$	$2\frac{2}{3}$
$\frac{14}{6}$	$\frac{12}{8}$	$2\frac{2}{6}$
$1\frac{4}{8}$	$\frac{8}{3}$	$5\frac{3}{5}$
$\frac{28}{5}$	$\frac{10}{3}$	$\frac{9}{2}$

Copyright © Big Ideas Learning, LLC.
All rights reserved.

Name ________________________________

Math Pennant

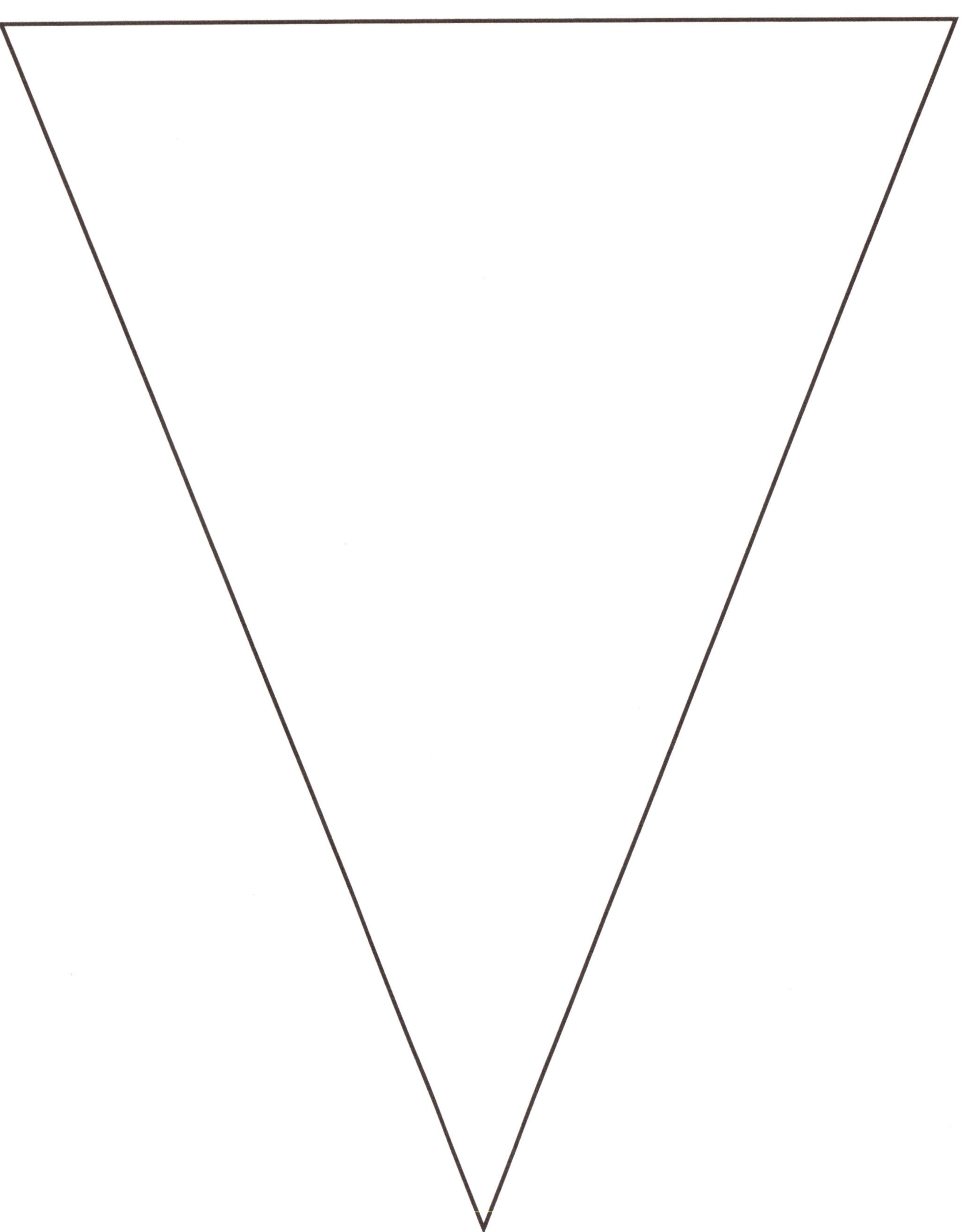

Copyright © Big Ideas Learning, LLC.
All rights reserved.

Name ______________________________

Measurement Cards

centimeters to millimeters	kilograms to grams	miles to feet
meters to centimeters	liters to milliliters	yards to inches
kilometers to meters	feet to inches	pounds to ounces
kilometers to centimeters	yards to feet	tons to pounds
meters to millimeters	miles to yards	

Copyright © Big Ideas Learning, LLC.
All rights reserved.

Name ______________________

Measurement Cards (continued)

pints to cups	minutes to seconds	years to weeks
quarts to pints	hours to minutes	days to seconds
gallons to quarts	days to hours	years to days
gallons to pints	weeks to days	days to minutes
quarts to cups	years to months	weeks to hours

Copyright © Big Ideas Learning, LLC.
All rights reserved.

Name ______________________________

Measurement Conversion Board Game

FINISH	FINISH
8 yd = ____ in.	12 gal = ____ pt
20 lb = ____ oz	8 m = ____ cm
11 km = ____ m	4 yd = ____ in.
23 L = ____ mL	5 mi = ____ ft
25 pt = ____ c	4 kg = ____ g
2 mi = ____ ft	15 lb = ____ oz
4 T = ____ lb	5 km = ____ m
4 m = ____ cm	1 wk = ____ h
7 kg = ____ g	40 L = ____ mL
3 wk = ____ d	6 T = ____ lb
START Player One	START Player Two

Copyright © Big Ideas Learning, LLC.
All rights reserved.

Name ______________________

Metric Conversion Flip and Find Cards

4 cm	40 mm	9 m	900 cm
5 km	5,000 m	3 kg	3,000 g
8 L	8,000 mL	2 m	200 cm
7 cm	70 mm	6 L	6,000 mL

Copyright © Big Ideas Learning, LLC.
All rights reserved.

Name ______________________________

Model Strategies Assessment

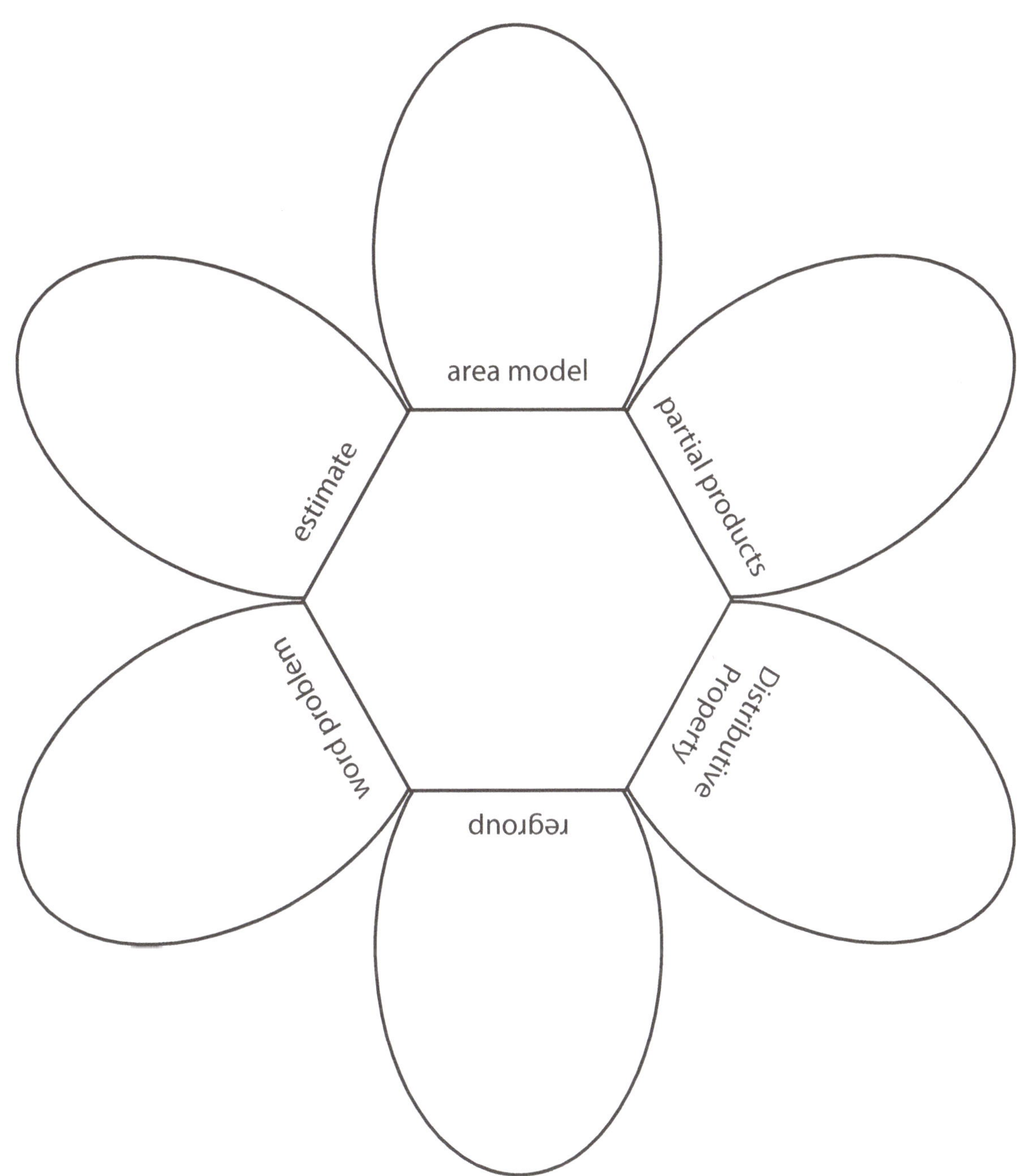

Copyright © Big Ideas Learning, LLC.
All rights reserved.

Name ___________________________

Money Cards

Copyright © Big Ideas Learning, LLC.
All rights reserved.

Name ______________________________

Money Match

penny	1¢	10 dimes	10¢
dollar	$1	100 pennies	100¢
quarter	25¢	25 cents	10 cents
nickel	5¢	5 cents	$\frac{1}{4}$ dollar
dime	$\frac{1}{10}$ dollar	$\frac{1}{100}$ dollar	1 cent

Copyright © Big Ideas Learning, LLC.
All rights reserved.

Name ______________________________

Money Place Value Mat

Money Amount	
Decimal	dollar
Fraction *OR* Mixed Number	dollar
Coins	

Copyright © Big Ideas Learning, LLC.
All rights reserved.

Name ______________________

Mosaic Grid

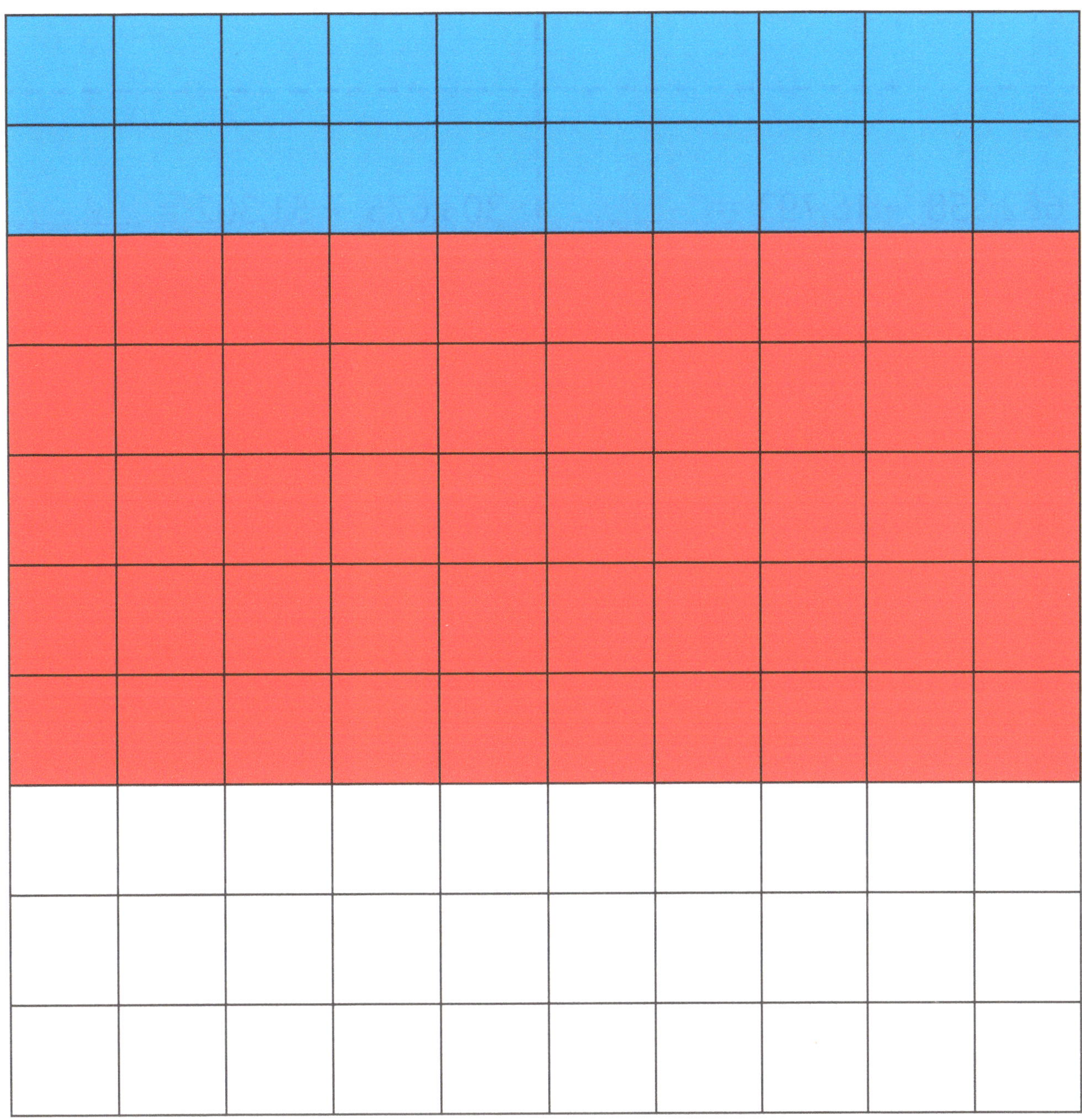

Copyright © Big Ideas Learning, LLC.
All rights reserved.

Name ______________________

Multi-Digit Strategy Problem Cards

72,341 − 38,025 = ______	64,629 + 47,586 = ______
682,558 − 15,793 = ______	303,675 + 51,302 = ______
407,256 − 29,376 = ______	677,943 + 28,486 = ______
968,743 − 82,535 = ______	814,321 + 16,068 = ______
549,631 − 228,371 = ______	750,296 + 124,475 = ______
645,942 − 452,520 = ______	379,521 + 356,849 = ______

Copyright © Big Ideas Learning, LLC.
All rights reserved.

Name ____________________

Multi-Digit Strategy Problem Cards (continued)

partial sums/differences	regrouping
partial sums/differences	regrouping
partial sums/differences	regrouping
compensation	counting on/back
compensation	counting on/back
compensation	counting on/back

Copyright © Big Ideas Learning, LLC.
All rights reserved.

Multiples of a Unit Fraction Picture Key

Name ________________________________

RED	
Expression	Product
$4 \times \frac{1}{10}$	
$4 \times \frac{1}{12}$	

ORANGE	
Expression	Product
$3 \times \frac{1}{6}$	
$4 \times \frac{1}{8}$	

BROWN	
Expression	Product
$2 \times \frac{1}{2}$	
$4 \times \frac{1}{4}$	
$3 \times \frac{1}{3}$	
$5 \times \frac{1}{5}$	

YELLOW	
Expression	Product
$6 \times \frac{1}{10}$	
$8 \times \frac{1}{12}$	

GREEN	
Expression	Product
$3 \times \frac{1}{6}$	
$4 \times \frac{1}{8}$	

Name ________________________________

RED	
Expression	Product
$4 \times \frac{1}{10}$	
$4 \times \frac{1}{12}$	

ORANGE	
Expression	Product
$3 \times \frac{1}{6}$	
$4 \times \frac{1}{8}$	

BROWN	
Expression	Product
$2 \times \frac{1}{2}$	
$4 \times \frac{1}{4}$	
$3 \times \frac{1}{3}$	
$5 \times \frac{1}{5}$	

YELLOW	
Expression	Product
$6 \times \frac{1}{10}$	
$8 \times \frac{1}{12}$	

GREEN	
Expression	Product
$3 \times \frac{1}{6}$	
$4 \times \frac{1}{8}$	

Copyright © Big Ideas Learning, LLC.
All rights reserved.

Name ____________________

Multiplication and Division Word Cards

× Multiplication ×

by	groups of
multiply	multiplied by
product	time
of	

Copyright © Big Ideas Learning, LLC.
All rights reserved.

Name ________________________

Multiplication and Division Word Cards (continued)

divide	equal parts
quotient	split
divided by	shared
per	

Copyright © Big Ideas Learning, LLC.
All rights reserved.

Name ______________________________

Multiplication Catcher

Directions: Cut along the solid lines. Fold along the dotted lines to create the Multiplication Strategy Catcher.

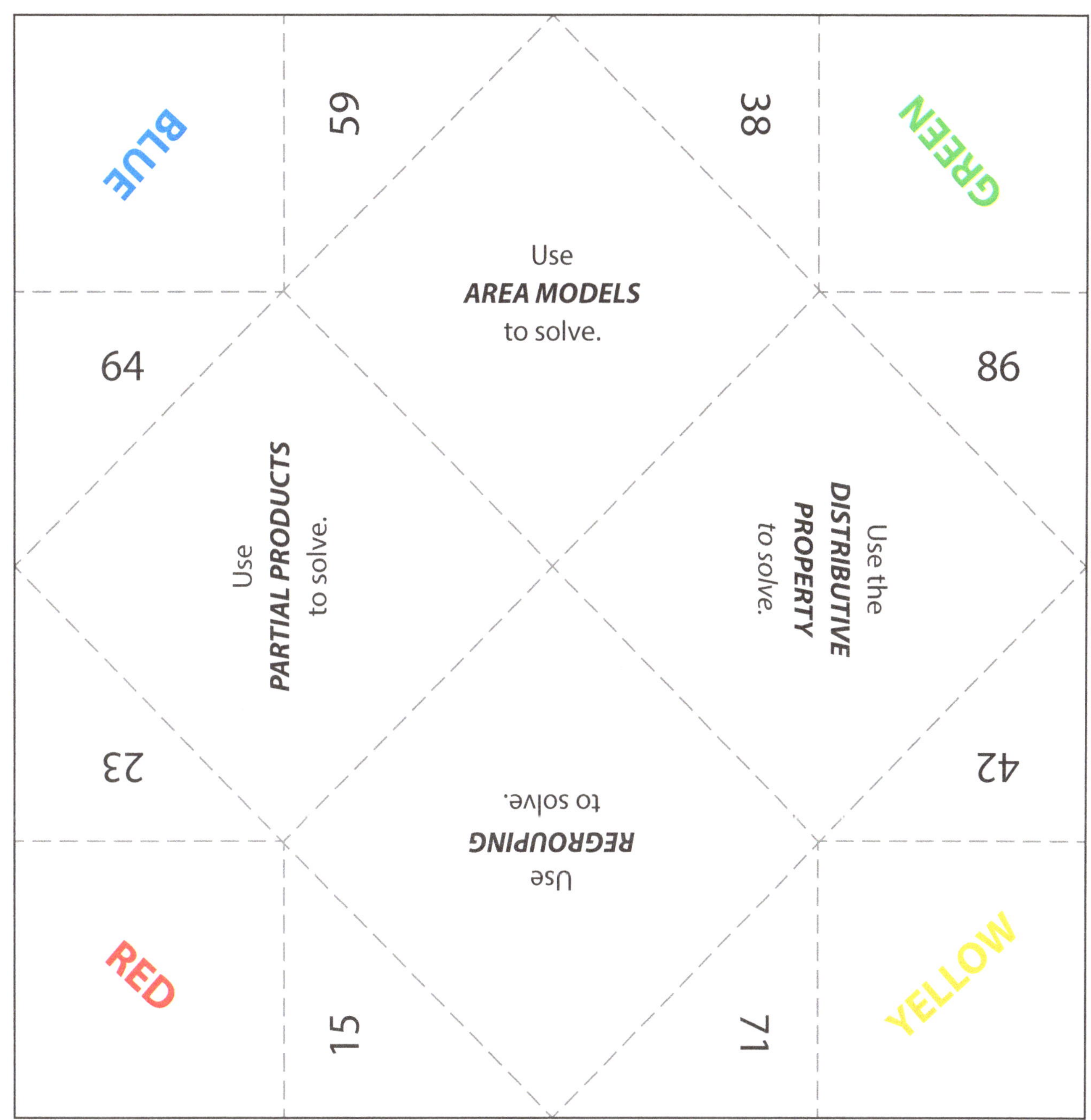

Copyright © Big Ideas Learning, LLC.
All rights reserved.

Name ____________________

Multiplication Puzzle

	Column 1	Column 2	Column 3
Row 1	top: 853 left: 9,426 right: 390 × 9 bottom: 401 × 8	top: 7,431 left: 3,510 right: 58 × 9 bottom: 1,249 × 3	top: 726 × 7 left: 522 right: 455 bottom: 2,903 × 5
Row 2	top: 3,208 left: 648 × 4 right: 5,955 bottom: 6 × 347	top: 3,747 left: 1,985 × 3 right: 408 × 7 bottom: 300	top: 14,515 left: 2,856 right: 29,974 bottom: 26 × 8
Row 3	top: 2,082 left: 7 × 510 right: 48 × 3 bottom: 4,610	top: 50 × 6 left: 144 right: 657 bottom: 3 × 4,267	top: 208 left: 73 × 9 right: 2,000 × 3 bottom: 16,326

Copyright © Big Ideas Learning, LLC.
All rights reserved.

Name ______________________________

Multiplication Pyramid Puzzle

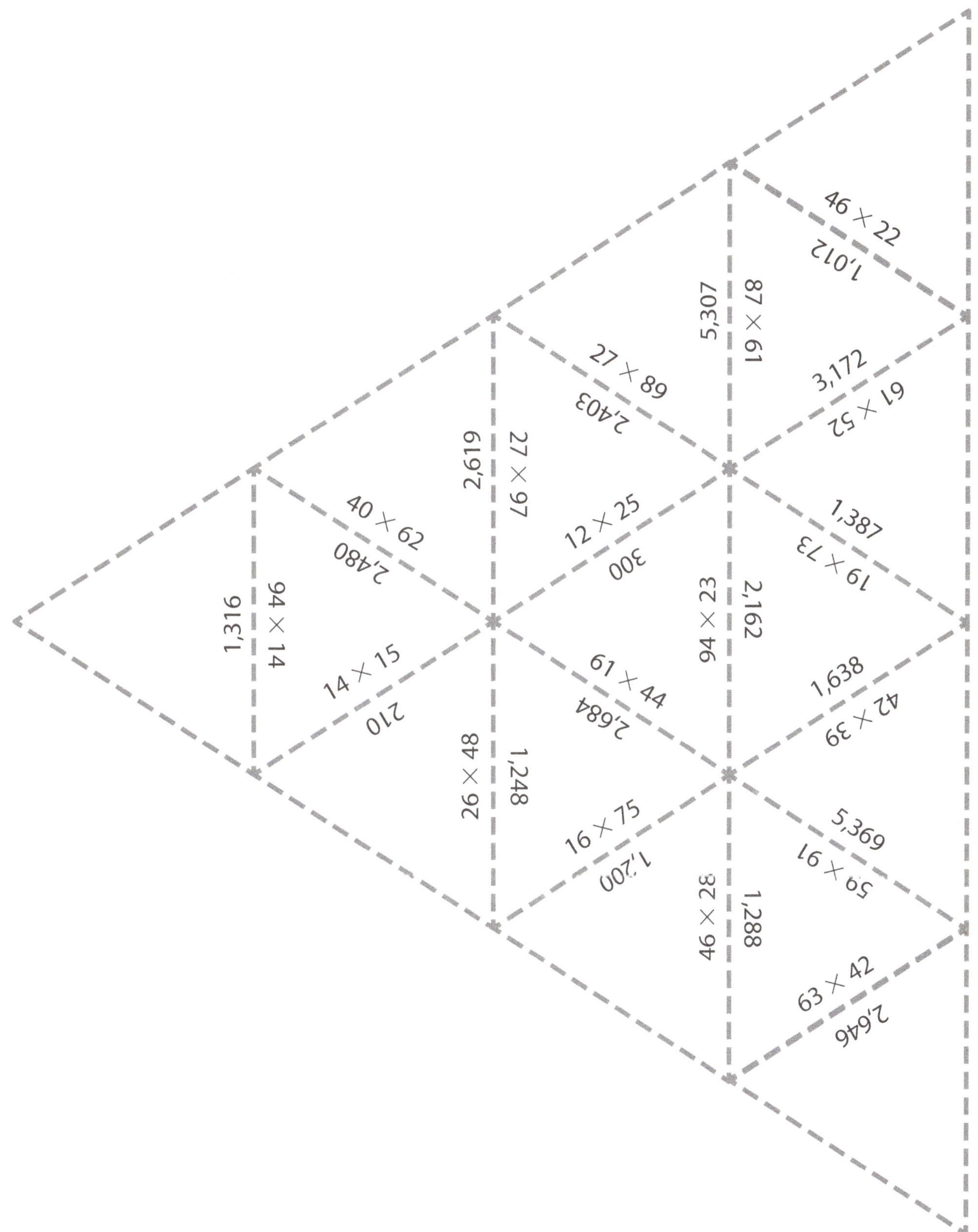

Copyright © Big Ideas Learning, LLC.
All rights reserved.

Name ______________________

Number Cards (0–9)

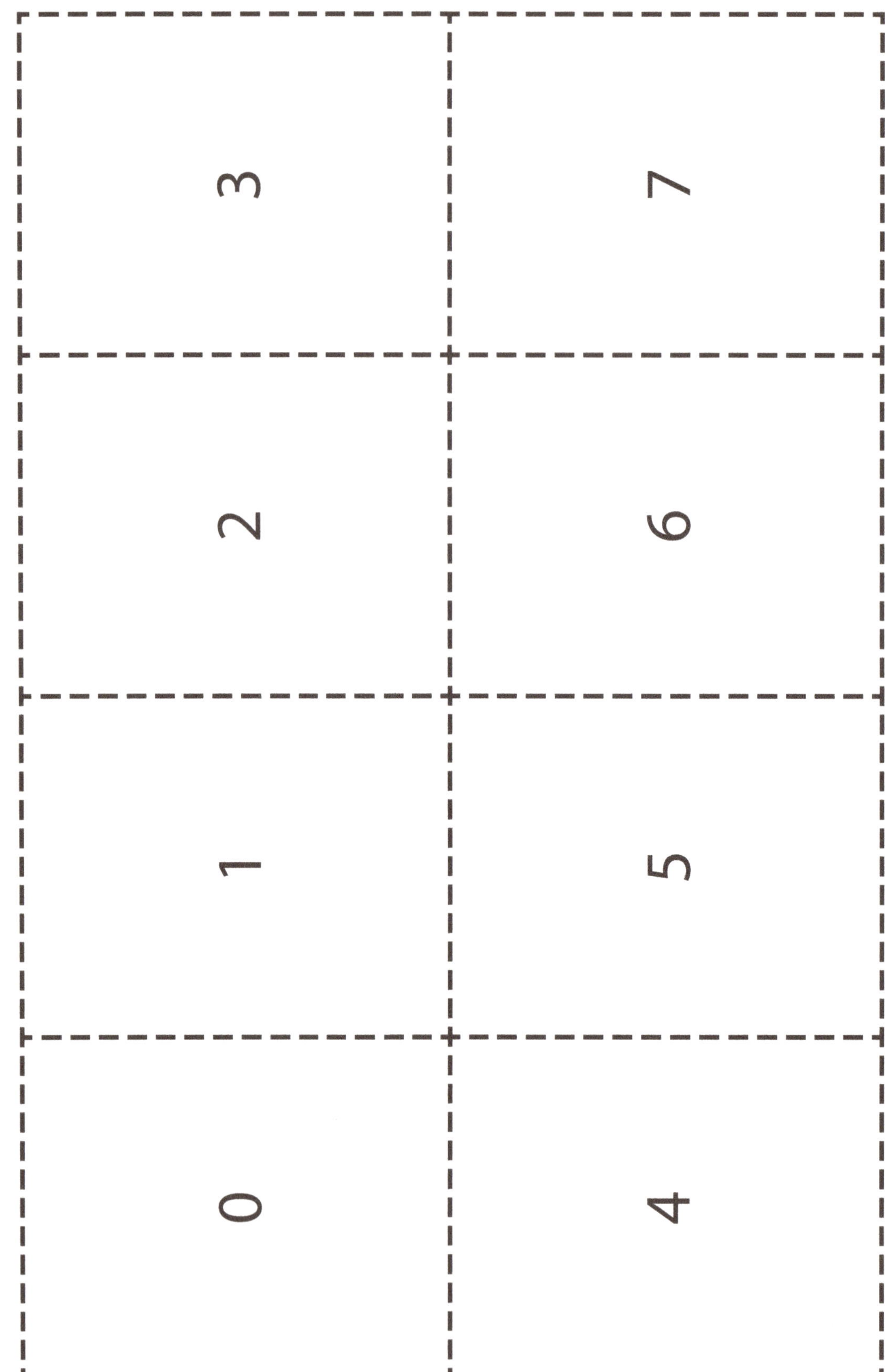

Copyright © Big Ideas Learning, LLC.
All rights reserved.

Name ______________________

Number Cards (0–9) (continued)

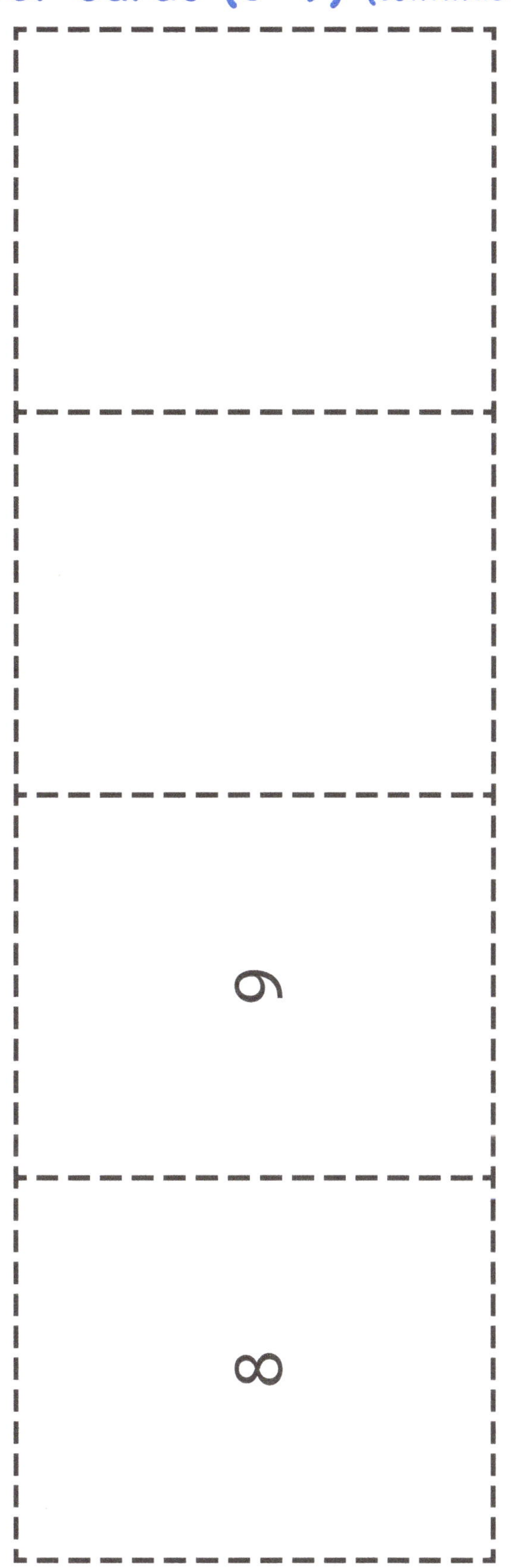

Copyright © Big Ideas Learning, LLC.
All rights reserved.

Number Lines

Name ______________________________

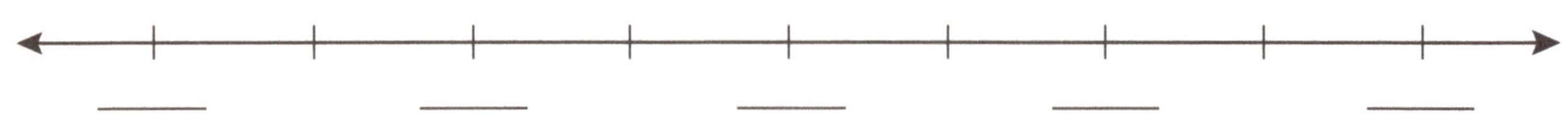

Name ______________________________

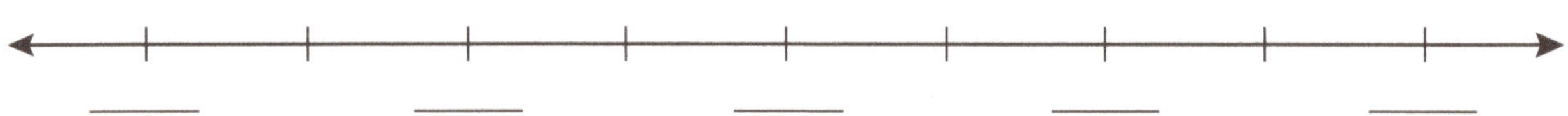

Name ______________________________

Name ______________________________

Copyright © Big Ideas Learning, LLC.
All rights reserved.

Pattern Blocks

Name ______________________________

Name ______________________________

Copyright © Big Ideas Learning, LLC.
All rights reserved.

Name ______________________________

Place Value Chart

Name ______________________________

Thousands Period			Ones Period		
Hundreds	Tens	Ones	Hundreds	Tens	Ones

Name ______________________________

Thousands Period			Ones Period		
Hundreds	Tens	Ones	Hundreds	Tens	Ones

Copyright © Big Ideas Learning, LLC.
All rights reserved.

Name ______________________________

Place Value Mat

Thousands	Hundreds	Tens	Ones

Copyright © Big Ideas Learning, LLC.
All rights reserved.

Name ______________________

Playground Checklist

Playground Equipemnt	Length	Width	Perimeter	Area
Spiral Slide	12 feet	7 feet		
Swings	8 feet	5 feet		
Rock Wall	4 feet	8 feet		
Twisty Round	6 feet	6 feet		
Game Court	11 feet	8 feet		
High Slide	15 feet	5 feet		
Equipment of choice			N/A	24 square feet
Equipment of choice			30 feet	N/A
Fence				N/A

Copyright © Big Ideas Learning, LLC.
All rights reserved.

Name ______________________________

Playground Checklist (continued)

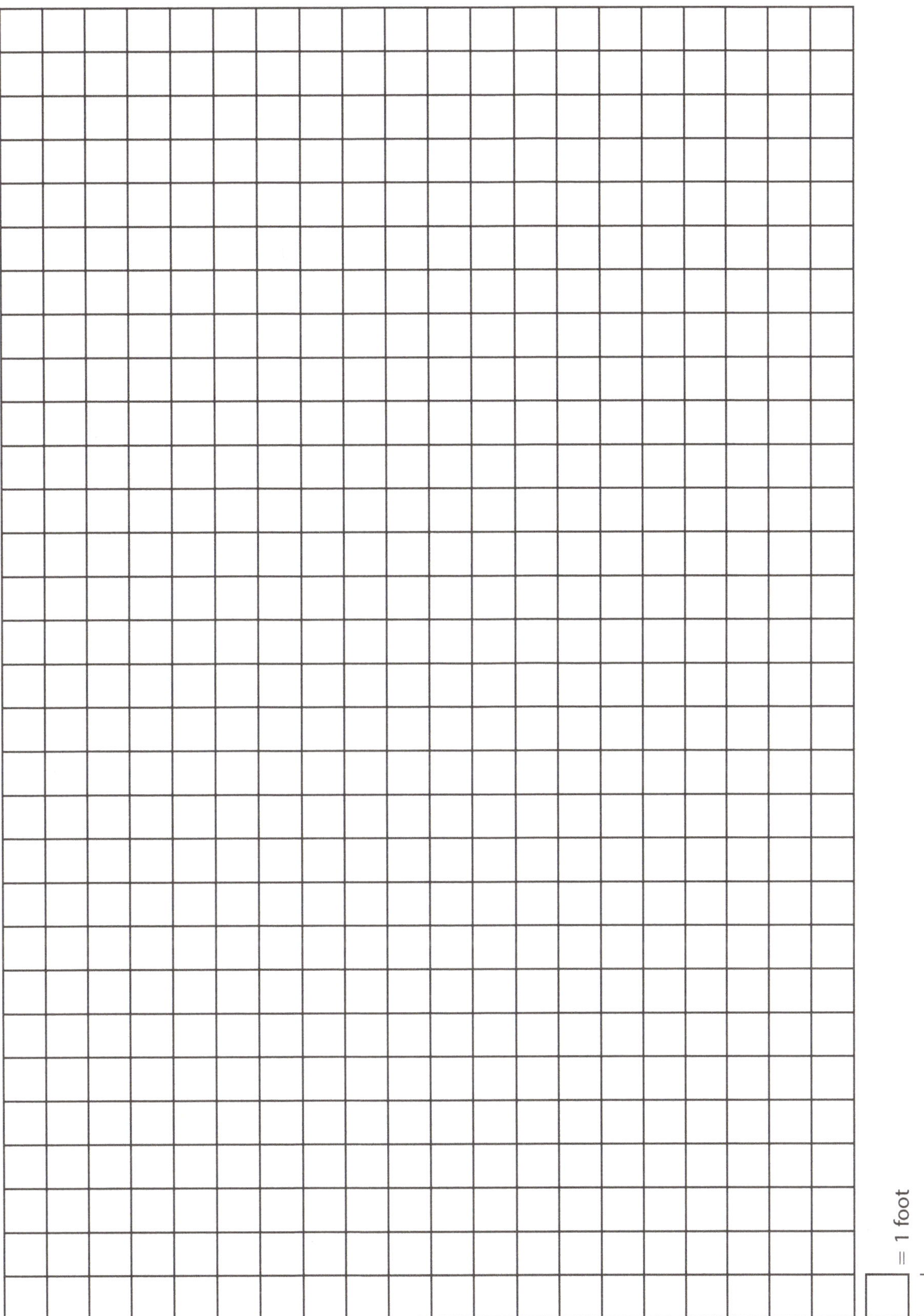

Copyright © Big Ideas Learning, LLC.
All rights reserved.

Name ______________________

Polygon Symmetry

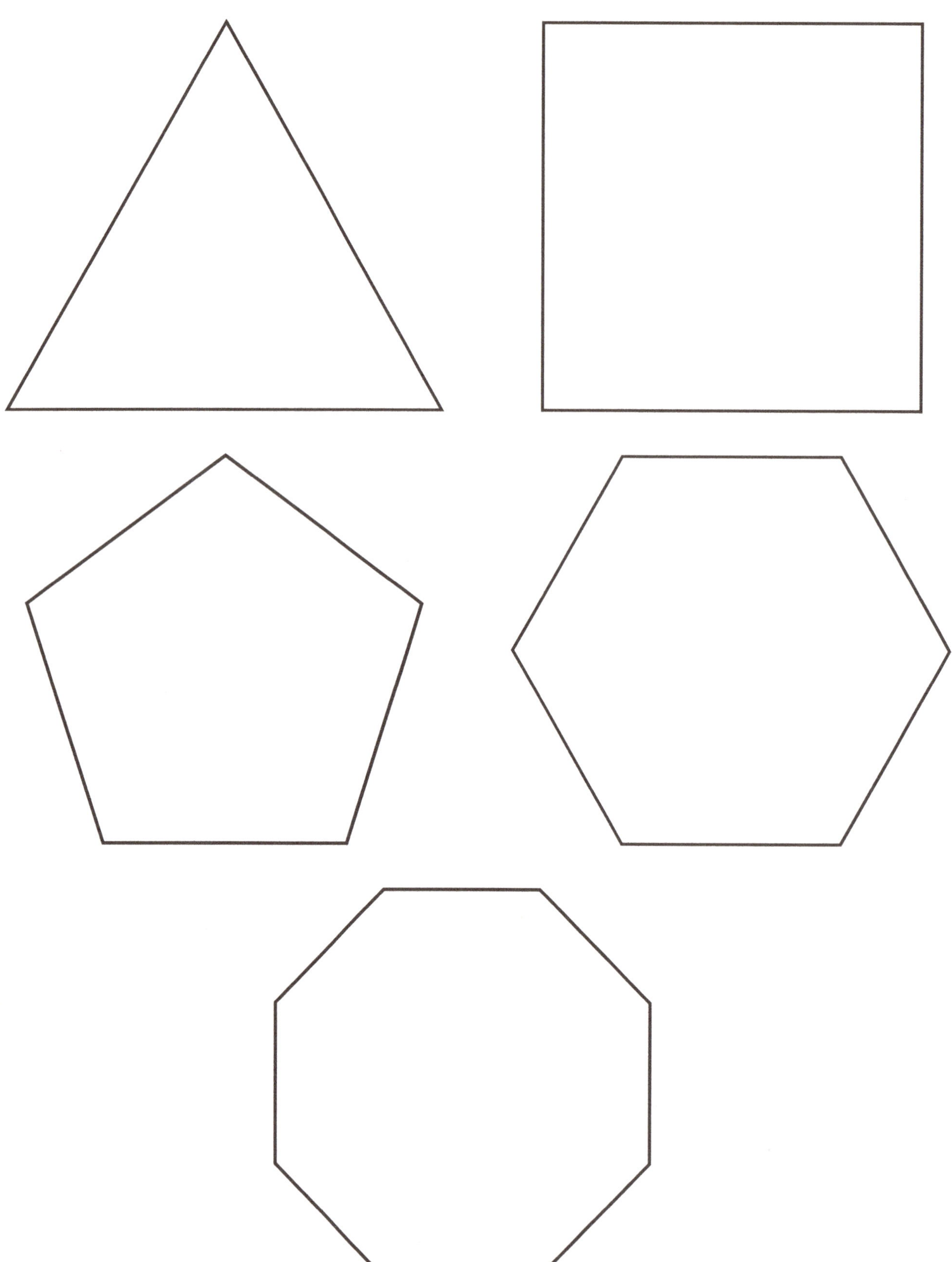

Copyright © Big Ideas Learning, LLC.
All rights reserved.

Name ______________________________

Prime and Composite Dots

Directions:

1. Players take turns spinning for a prime number or composite number.
2. On your turn, connect two dots that border a number that matches your spin. Use a different color than your partner.
3. If you close a square, color it in. If you do not close a square, your turn is over.
4. Continue playing until all of the prime numbers and composite numbers are colored.
5. The player with the most colored squares wins!

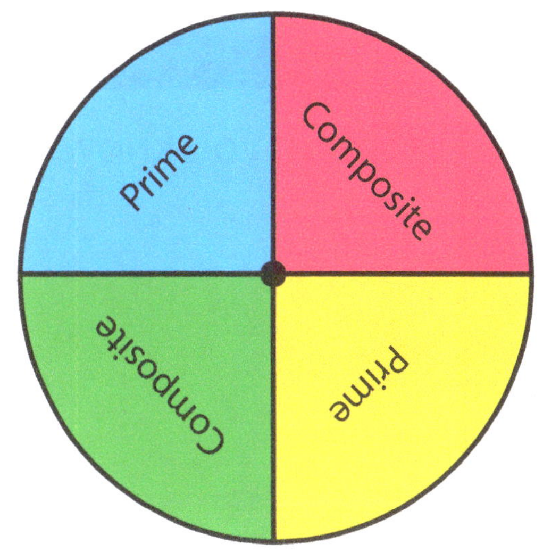

89	15	91	7
52	31	47	84
71	27	13	44
9	39	29	63

Copyright © Big Ideas Learning, LLC.
All rights reserved.

Name ______________________

Problem-Solving Plan

Understand the Problem

What do you know?	What do you need to find?

Make a Plan

How will you solve?

Solve

Copyright © Big Ideas Learning, LLC.
All rights reserved.

Name ______________________

Quadrilateral Corner

Copyright © Big Ideas Learning, LLC.
All rights reserved.

Name ______________________

Race for the Moon Cards

4,921 + 28,674 = _□,___	2,498 + 7,507 = __,_□_	60,435 + 6,992 = __,_□_
57,204 + 378,087 = ___,__□	88,109 + 7,231 = __,_□_	520,731 + 179,642 = ___,__□
226,438 + 581,372 = _□_,___	65,927 + 382,104 = □__,___	719,250 + 98,715 = _□_,___
97,341 + 651,860 = ___,□__	256,189 + 134,242 = ___,□__	403,956 + 20,389 = _□_,___

Copyright © Big Ideas Learning, LLC.
All rights reserved.

Name ______________________

Race for the Moon Cards (continued)

527,319 − 43,734 _ _ □, _ _ _	719,648 − 328,937 _ _ _, _ □ _	63,470 − 51,982 □ _, _ _ _
406,257 − 392,638 _ _ □, _ _ _	88,346 − 27,953 _ □, _ _ _	686,794 − 68,725 _ _ _, □ _ _
952,015 − 237,923 _ □ _, _ _ _	294,623 − 53,407 □ _ _, _ _ _	73,598 − 644 _ _, _ _ □
8,631 − 4,424 _, □ _ _	7,319 − 4,671 _, _ □ _	48,090 − 9,856 _ _, _ □ _

Copyright © Big Ideas Learning, LLC.
All rights reserved.

Name ______________________

Remainder Takes All

Directions:

1. Players take turns covering a number on the game board with a counter.
2. On your turn, cover a number and roll the dice.
3. Divide the number you covered by the number on the dice. The remainder is your score.
4. The student with the highest score at the end of 10 rounds wins!

517	214	6,941	84	745	370
618	51	407	8,215	117	589
905	4,822	658	814	300	49
5,759	731	898	3,189	64	7,777
376	412	974	6,380	52	847
248	93	768	400	5,249	870

Copyright © Big Ideas Learning, LLC.
All rights reserved.

Name ____________________

Remainder Takes All Recording Sheet

	Player 1	Player 2
Round 1		
Round 2		
Round 3		
Round 4		
Round 5		
Round 6		
Round 7		
Round 8		
Round 9		
Round 10		
Total		

Copyright © Big Ideas Learning, LLC.
All rights reserved.

Name ______________________________

Roll to Compare Decimals Recording Sheet

Round	Player 1 Tallies: ____________	Player 2 Tallies: ____________
1	___.___ ___	___.___ ___
2	___.___ ___	___.___ ___
3	___.___ ___	___.___ ___
4	___.___ ___	___.___ ___
5	___.___ ___	___.___ ___
6	___.___ ___	___.___ ___
7	___.___ ___	___.___ ___
8	___.___ ___	___.___ ___
9	___.___ ___	___.___ ___
10	___.___ ___	___.___ ___

Copyright © Big Ideas Learning, LLC.
All rights reserved.

Name ______________________________

Rounding and Solving

Directions:

1. Players take turns rolling a die and creating a 6-digit number.
2. On your turn, record the number in your Actual Number box.
3. With your partner, round your number to the nearest hundred, thousand, and ten thousand.
4. Work with your partner to find the sum or difference of each column.

	Actual Number	Nearest Hundred	Nearest Thousand	Nearest Ten Thousand
Player 1	___,___	___,___	___,___	___,___
Player 2	___,___	___,___	___,___	___,___
Sum	___,___	___,___	___,___	___,___

	Actual Number	Nearest Hundred	Nearest Thousand	Nearest Ten Thousand
Player 1	___,___	___,___	___,___	___,___
Player 2	___,___	___,___	___,___	___,___
Sum	___,___	___,___	___,___	___,___

Copyright © Big Ideas Learning, LLC.
All rights reserved.

Name ______________________________

Search for Someone Who Can...

Directions: Find a different classmate to complete and initial each box.

Round 285,938 to the nearest ten. initials: _____	Round 402,894 to the nearest hundred. initials: _____	Round 42,159 to the nearest thousand. initials: _____	Round 6,290 to the nearest thousand. initials: _____
Round 229,132 to the nearest hundred thousand. initials: _____	Round 894,265 to the nearest ten. initials: _____	Round 402,917 to the nearest hundred. initials: _____	Round 405,913 to the nearest hundred. initials: _____
Round 29,341 to the nearest hundred. initials: _____	Round 7,428 to the nearest thousand. initials: _____	Round 57,021 to the nearest ten thousand. initials: _____	Round 648,254 to the nearest ten thousand. initials: _____
Round 41,926 to the nearest ten thousand. initials: _____	Round 148,765 to the nearest ten. initials: _____	Round 137,208 to the nearest hundred thousand. initials: _____	Round 79,439 to the nearest ten. initials: _____

Copyright © Big Ideas Learning, LLC.
All rights reserved.

Name ______________________________

Skate Around the Rink

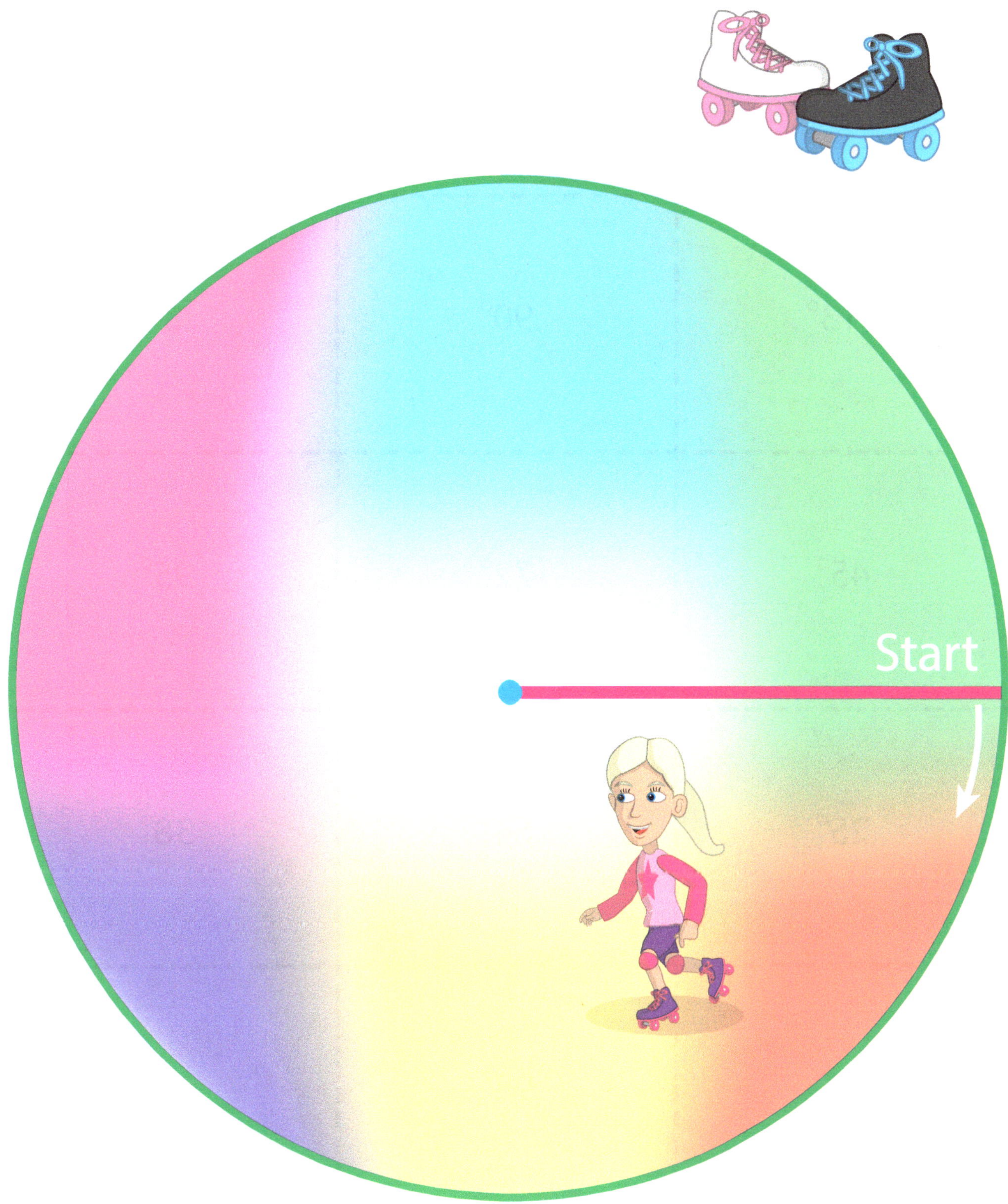

Copyright © Big Ideas Learning, LLC.
All rights reserved.

Name ________________________________

Skate Around the Rink (continued)

10°	30°	15°
113°	90°	8°
45°	72°	95°
25°	64°	38°
60°	98°	5°

Copyright © Big Ideas Learning, LLC.
All rights reserved.

Name ____________________

Spoons Cards

4×30	3×40	2×60	6×20
$1 \times 1{,}600$	200×8	2×800	400×4
6×30	3×60	2×90	9×20

Copyright © Big Ideas Learning, LLC.
All rights reserved.

Name ______________________

Spoons Cards (continued)

60×4	40×6	8×30	3×80
$3 \times 1,000$	5×600	6×500	$2 \times 500 \times 3$
360×1	$3 \times 40 \times 3$	4×90	6×60

Copyright © Big Ideas Learning, LLC.
All rights reserved.

Name ______________________

Spoons Cards (continued)

5×800	500×8	$4 \times 1{,}000$	$2{,}000 \times 2$
3×20	30×2	60×1	10×6
10×10	5×20	2×50	$2 \times 25 \times 2$

Copyright © Big Ideas Learning, LLC.
All rights reserved.

Name ______________________

Spoons Cards (continued)

80×7	7×80	$4 \times 2 \times 70$	8×70
70×3	3×70	30×7	7×30
60×8	$4 \times 60 \times 2$	1×480	80×6

Copyright © Big Ideas Learning, LLC.
All rights reserved.

Name ______________________

Spoons Cards (continued)

2×70	20×7	70×2	7×20
$3 \times 3{,}000$	$9 \times 1{,}000$	$1 \times 9{,}000$	$1{,}000 \times 3 \times 3$
8×40	80×4	$80 \times 2 \times 2$	40×8

Copyright © Big Ideas Learning, LLC.
All rights reserved.

Name ______________________

Summary Triangle Graphic Organizer

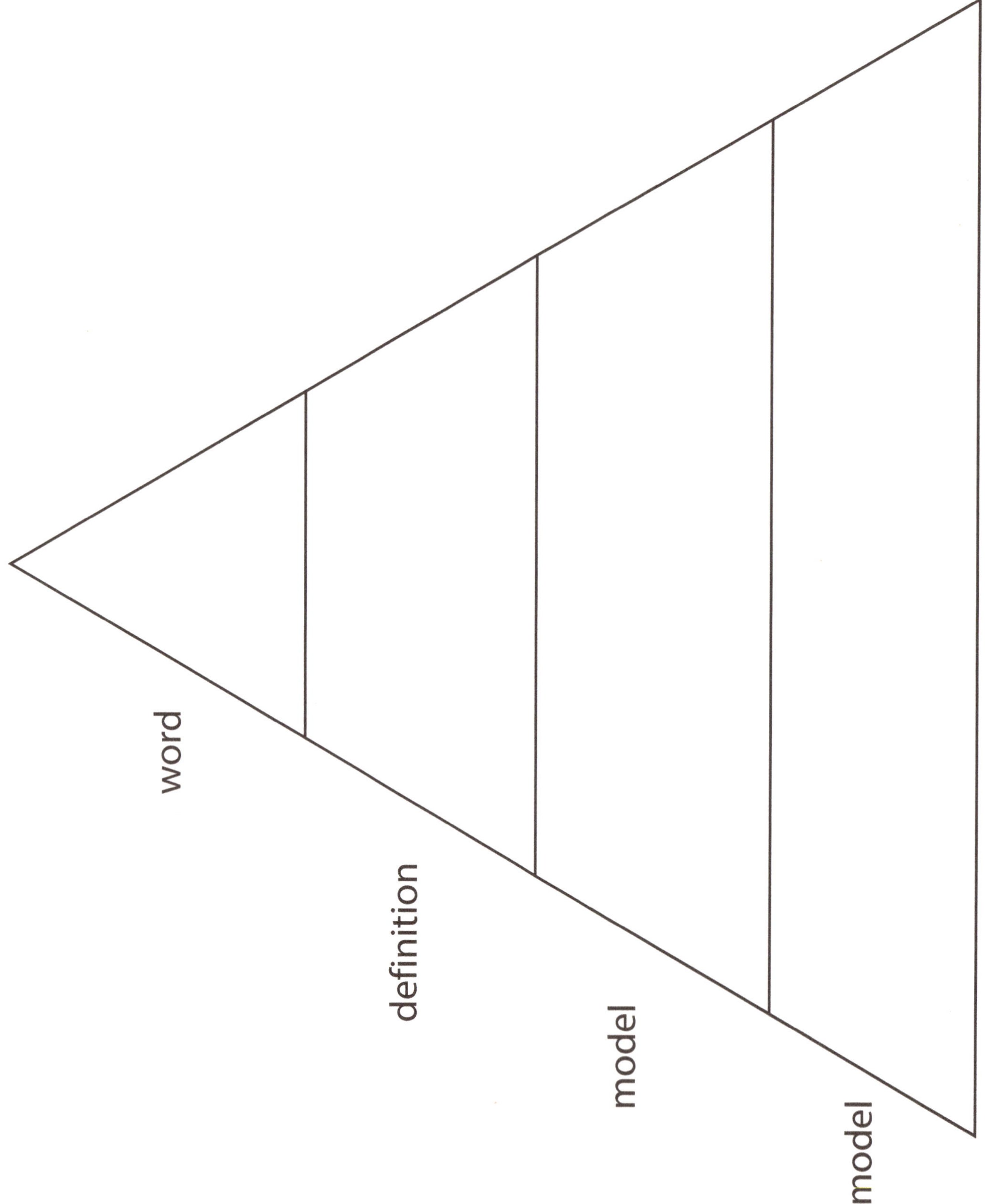

Copyright © Big Ideas Learning, LLC.
All rights reserved.

Name ______________________

Time Conversion Flip and Find Cards

5 min	300 sec	6 h	360 min
3 d	72 h	9 wk	63 d
4 yr	48 mo	2 yr	104 wk
8 min	480 sec	7 wk	49 d

Copyright © Big Ideas Learning, LLC.
All rights reserved.

Name ______________________

Two-Digit Four in a Row

Directions:

1. Players take turns flipping cards.
2. On your turn, solve the multiplication problem on the Two-Digit Four in a Row Card. Cover the product with a counter.
3. The first player to create a line of four in a row, horizontally, vertically, or diagonally, wins!

5,880	750	4,700	960
1,440	3,520	2,610	3,920
720	3,100	1,500	1,740
3,710	2,700	840	3,320

Copyright © Big Ideas Learning, LLC.
All rights reserved.

Name ______________________

Two-Digit Four in a Row Cards

40×21	50×62	60×29	90×30
20×36	50×94	80×12	30×48
10×75	30×87	70×56	40×83
60×98	80×44	70×53	20×75

Copyright © Big Ideas Learning, LLC.
All rights reserved.

Name ____________________

Venn Diagram Graphic Organizer

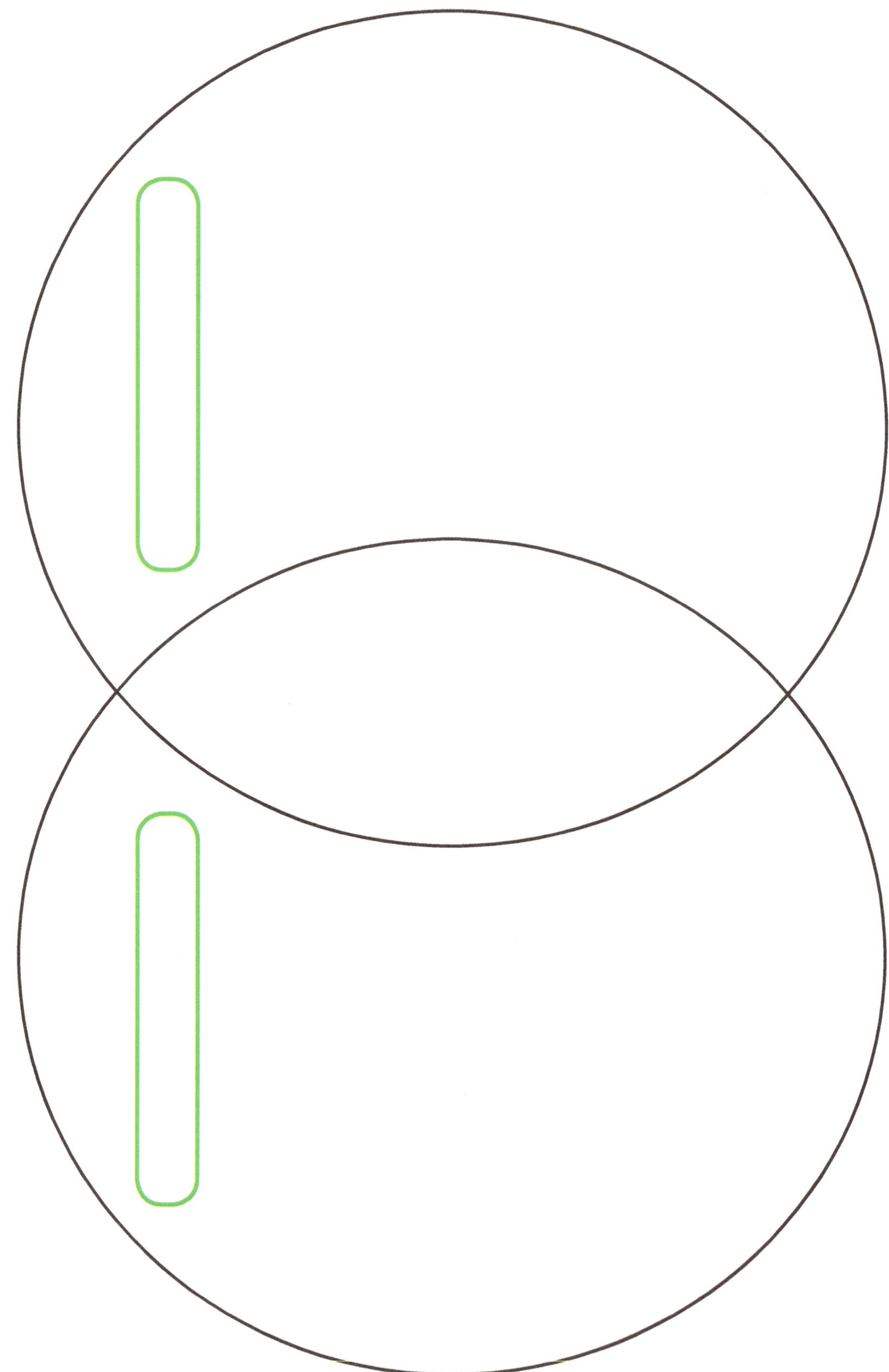

Copyright © Big Ideas Learning, LLC.
All rights reserved.

Name ______________________________

Web Graphic Organizer

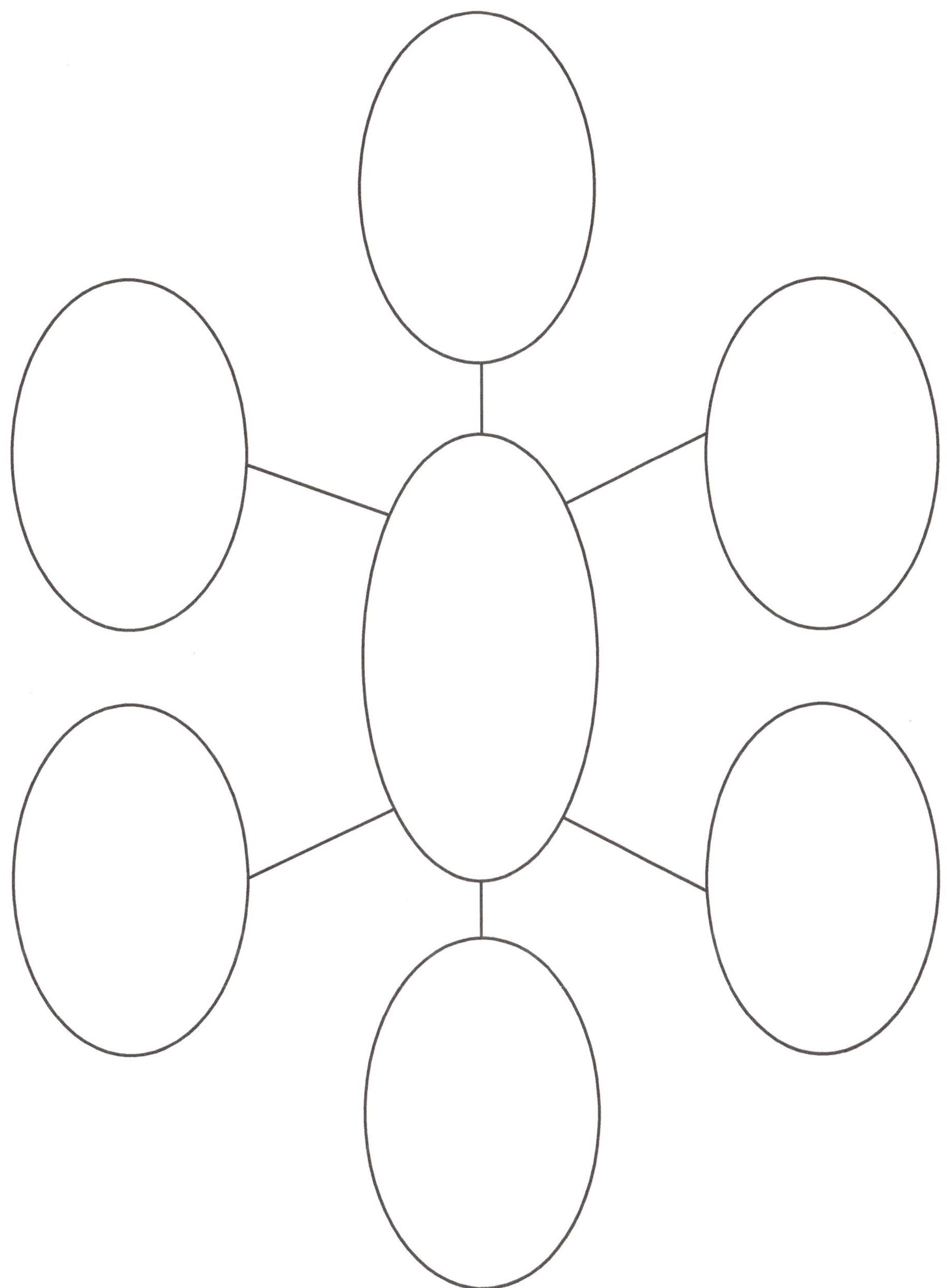

Copyright © Big Ideas Learning, LLC.
All rights reserved.

Name ______________________

Word Problem Match Up

A football league has 23 teams. Each team has 35 players. How many players are in the league?

805

players

25 apples are picked every day from each tree in an orchard. There are 78 trees in the orchard. How many apples are picked in one day?

1,950

apples

There are 17 levels in a game. Each level has 84 coins. How many coins are there in the game?

1,428

coins

Your school is holding a muffin sale. Each family brings in one dozen (12) muffins. 68 families participate. How many muffins are there?

816

muffins

Copyright © Big Ideas Learning, LLC.
All rights reserved.

Name ____________________

Word Problem Match Up (continued)

A fourth grade class is holding a fundraiser to go a science center. Each of the 53 students needs to raise $42. How much money does the trip cost?	A city wants to plant 28 trees at each of the 15 city parks. How many trees do they need?
2,226	420
dollars	trees

Copyright © Big Ideas Learning, LLC.
All rights reserved.

Name ______________________

Writing Multi-Digit Numbers

three thousand, four hundred thirty-two	56,902
one hundred six thousand, ninety-seven	816,423
four hundred sixteen thousand, eighty-seven	134,078
fifty-three thousand, twenty-nine	36,580
700,000 + 50,000 + 8,000 + 20 + 9	400,000 + 20,000 + 500 + 60 + 1
30,000 + 1,000 + 400 + 20 + 8	800,000 + 30,000 + 1,000 + 300 + 90 + 5

Copyright © Big Ideas Learning, LLC.
All rights reserved.